"I Destroyed Cancer Today.

What Did you Do?"

A Father's Memoir

By Jim Dezell

© 2022, Jim Dezell, All Rights Reserved

This book is dedicated in memory of Kelvin Thomas, Brooke Hester, Cole Stoddard and Angie Murray: May they continue to be angels looking after those impacted by childhood cancer and shepherding the eradication of this illness.

It is also dedicated to the women and men (including Dr. Jennifer Levine and Dr. Prakash Satwani) who are researching and delivering cures for pediatric cancer. May you continue to be guided medically, scientifically and spiritually in this pursuit.

© 2022, Jim Dezell, All Rights Reserved

INTRODUCTION/FORWARD

When people describe a devastating life event, they often recall feeling "as if all the oxygen had been sucked out of the room."

When your child is diagnosed with cancer, the reaction is even more intense. The Earth itself stops moving. Your life doesn't just stall, it hits a brick wall. Sunshine and beautiful days do not matter. The stress is all consuming and relentless. Everything you thought, felt, aspire to and planned falls into limbo. The momentum of your entire existence ceases. This book is about how our family initially encountered my son's cancer and our journey back to sanity. But, then, the cancer returned, and we had to combat it all over again.

This is about our odyssey. It is a narrative by a father and husband—recalling how we as a family conquered cancer. Twice.

It is accompanied by portions of a CaringBridge blog that my wife, Keri, created during the treatments to chronicle our family's experience through our son's battle with cancer. Some responses to Keri's blog posts are also listed because they are so inspiring.

Cancer is brutal, ugly, sneaky, unrelenting and disgusting. I describe how we used perseverance, insanity, laughter, love and spirituality to defeat it.

At times, sections of the book are raw, frightening and alarming. Cancer is all of that, too, which is why I didn't shy away from this tone.

My motivation for writing the book is simple: It may help someone with a life-threatening disease, or families on a similar journey. By no means do I (or my family) feel that we have all the answers to fighting cancer or how to address it. We do believe, however, that we were spiritually guided and influenced by a higher power in how to deal with it.

I tell our story from a father's perspective as it unfolded. It is also an unabashed tribute to a courageous and an inspirational young man: Frankie Dezell.

Our hope is that we help others gain insight and strength from any of the extraordinary experiences our family survived.

Proceeds from the sale of this book will be donated to The Morgan Stanley Children's Hospital at Columbia University in New York, to the continued research and development of Dr. Satwani's work for pediatric cancer patients in India, and to the Lil' Bravest Foundation in Washington Heights, NY.

The First 24 Hours: "The Numbness Period"

The day started quite frenetically: kids going to school, my commute to work, afterschool homework and an evening trumpet recital. It was our normal, daily chaos.

Then, out of nowhere, it all stopped. It was 5 p.m. on May 20, 2010. We were suddenly in the pediatric oncology clinic at Columbia University's Morgan Stanley Children's Hospital in New York City, trying to make sense of our world.

I remember sitting on a rolling stool that had a broken back. It was uncomfortable because the backrest kept shifting all over the place. Every time I tried to sit up straight or lean backward, the backrest would move so there was nothing to support me. I had no idea how symbolic that stool would become.

When I first got to the hospital that afternoon, I was dazed and in shock. The day before, our hometown pediatrician had run blood tests on our 8-year-old son, Frankie. A couple of days earlier, Frankie had had a fever, some difficulty breathing and bruising. The pediatrician called that morning and asked my wife, Keri, to return to his office. He gently directed her to sit down and told her that the bloodwork indicated Frankie had cancer.

Keri frantically called me at work to share the test results. I was in disbelief and insisted on a second opinion. Hours later, we found ourselves sitting at Columbia University's clinic in Manhattan. The walls were painted in a boorish, drab color. The nurses' station was a pale, muted blue. About a dozen other young cancer patients were waiting with their families. Floor to ceiling curtains surrounded most of the chairs in the clinic, to give patients some semblance of privacy. The curtains were dreary and threadbare. To shift my attention from the hospital's gloomy décor, I kept staring out the windows at the Hudson River and the George Washington Bridge. Frankie watched some cartoons on the television.

Before I arrived, aides had taken some additional blood samples from Frankie. About 90 minutes later, a nurse approached us and pulled me aside. She handed me a printout of the blood test. It consisted of a three-column chart of symptoms. I studied it intently. One column identified what are "Normal" readings; the second listed Frankie's blood results; in the third column, the variances from "Normal" were shaded. The chart detailed white blood counts, platelets, hemoglobin levels and other findings. The differences between my son's levels and what was classified as "Normal" were staggering.

"These are the classic indicators of leukemia," the nurse gently explained, pointing at the white blood cell stats. She added: "The platelet levels are also rather low."

I was silent for a moment and then slowly rolled back on the broken stool. After a while, the nurse looked at me. "Are you okay?"

I sighed and looked at the ceiling "Yeah, I'm okay," I replied. "And I thought my biggest problem today was missing the 8:10 train."

As the afternoon made way to evening, Frankie, Keri and I were shuffled across various floors and moved in and out of multiple hospital rooms. Columbia's facilities in New York City have been around for over 150 years. The complex is a massive structure and almost a city unto itself. We were asked to sign tons of paperwork and were introduced to several doctors and nurses assigned to take on Frankie's case.

While waiting in one of the rooms, my mind momentarily shut out the commotion and imagery around me. I began recalling that just a couple of weeks before, I had thrown out a donation request I had received from the Leukemia & Lymphoma Society. *I don't know anyone with leukemia*, I thought, and discarded the envelope with pictures of bald children on the outside of it.

I remembered that less than a week before, I was at a carnival with my kids...watching Frankie summon his courage to get on the "Alibaba"—a ride he had seen only older kids handle. And the day before, Frankie was at his first lacrosse game, but he had to pull himself out of it because of difficulty breathing. I learned later that the cancer was depleting him of his oxygen-rich red blood cells.

Initially, we thought that Frankie wasn't feeling well because of allergies, or maybe he had developed asthma like one of his older brothers. Worst case scenario: It was Lyme disease.

We never could have fathomed that Frankie had cancer.

Hospital staff finally moved us to the pediatric oncology area of the hospital and put us in a temporary room for a few hours until another one was ready. We told Frankie that because he didn't feel well, we were going to have some tests done and spend the night at the hospital. He accepted that explanation and exchanged banter with the doctors and nurses. Many of them asked about sports and heard of his loyalty to Boston-area teams (which didn't sit well with the rival New Yorkers). I kept joking and teasing with Frankie to keep him relaxed.

About 9 p.m., I remembered that my brother John from Philadelphia was expected at our house in suburban New York the next day to help with some electrical work. I found a quiet corner of the hospital floor to call him and postpone the visit.

"Hey, you ready to pull some wires tomorrow?" he began.

"I don't think that's going to happen, John," I replied. "Frankie hasn't felt well all week. We are at the hospital...."

"Does he have the flu?" he interjected. "There's a nasty bout of that going around...."

"No, John. It is a lot more complicated than that. They ran some tests." I started to whisper and was getting choked up. "He had a low-grade fever that spiked this week and isn't going down. They ended up doing bloodwork because we thought it might be Lyme disease. The results came back...it isn't Lyme. My little boy has leukemia."

I recall feeling terribly alone as I said that—as if we were on a planet so far removed from reality. It was a planet that no one we knew had ever landed on. My brother simply replied, "Oh my

God, Jim."

About 10:30 p.m., we finally got Frankie into his own hospital room. I lingered to make sure he wasn't nervous as Keri prepared to stay overnight, sleeping on a futon in his room that could be converted into a sofa during the day.

My mind was in a fog as I drove the 40 miles to our home north of the city, arriving at 2 a.m. Keri had contacted her parents in Massachusetts to tell them the devastating news, so my in-laws had driven from the Boston area to stay with our other two sons, James and Max, who were then ages 12 and 10. I woke up early that morning and got breakfast set up. Our oldest son, James, woke up first and bounced into the kitchen before school.

"Oh hi, Dad!" he began. "Who is with Frankie?"

"Your mom," I replied.

"So, they are doing tests on him. They think he has Lyme disease?"

I poured his cereal and suggested that he sit, eat it and take his vitamin. His grandfather was standing behind me. James again asked, "Is it Lyme disease?"

We live in a heavily wooded suburb and, given the prevalence of deer in our area, ticks and Lyme disease are common. I leaned over the kitchen counter and propped up my head. My face was about a foot away as James ate his cereal.

"They did run tests, James. Unfortunately, it is not Lyme."

He looked up at me and became distraught. He knew by my demeanor that what I was about to say next was going to be shattering.

"James, your brother was diagnosed with leukemia last night."

The color in his face drained quickly. His eyes filled with tears. They began pouring down his face and dropping into his cereal bowl.

"You mean he has cancer?! Frankie has cancer?"
I nodded slowly.

"Oh my God. Oh my God. This is horrible. Is he going to die?"

From the moment we found out about Frankie's cancer, I never let my mind dwell on death or dying. It was not a matter of being macho at all, but the word "die"—along with "death," "dying," "passing" and so on—irked me. As far as I was concerned, *it was never going to happen*. I was immediately annoyed when it was brought up. However, I was sympathetic to James' fears and didn't reveal my frustration.

"No, James, he is not going to die," I answered firmly.

"But people who get cancer die," James implored. "It kills them..."

I stood up and started pacing.

"Your brother is not going to die, James. And let me explain why. Cancer thrives off feelings of weakness and vulnerability. Cancer wants to make you feel afraid. Well, guess what? We are not weak, and we are not scared..."

James stopped crying and stared at me.

"We will destroy this, James. Frankie will destroy this." I continued to pace across the kitchen. "We are very tough people, James. And this is a tough family."

Our entire conversation started to sink in and then James began sobbing uncontrollably. "Why is it Frankie who is sick? I wish it was me who was sick." I had to provide further reassurance.

"Let me explain to you, James, that Frankie is at Columbia University's hospital. These are some of the greatest doctors in the world, James."

He stopped sobbing, but his eyes were welled with tears. He was panicked, and I knew that he needed some consolation on the diagnosis, the situation, the doctors, and the hospital. My mind raced to find the simplest way to convince him. I knew I could get my point across if I referenced the National Football League. I leaned back and came up with a game plan:

"James," I said, "these doctors at Columbia are the 'Tom Brady's of doctors'...these are the best of the best. We will crush this illness."

My father-in-law drove James to school. An hour later, our

middle son, Max, came downstairs for breakfast and we had a similar conversation about Frankie. His reactions and emotions were identical to his brother's. I looked him in the eyes and assured him that we were collectively going to help Frankie beat this. I then hugged him tight and took him to school.

The Next 24 Hours: "The Anger Period"

Once we had taken care of Max and James, I worked from home to sort out and organize matters. Then I headed back to the hospital about 3 p.m. Amidst the chaos of the previous 24 hours, we still hadn't told Frankie of the cancer diagnosis (only that more tests were needed).

We learned that one of the many grisly ways doctors treat and monitor leukemia—a cancer of the blood and bone marrow caused by the rapid production of abnormal white blood cells—is to perform multiple spinal taps: They insert a needle into the spine to collect fluid to check for cancer and then use a different needle to inject chemo drugs into the spine to prevent the cancer from entering the spinal column/brain. A similar procedure—bone marrow aspiration—would be needed to check Frankie's bone marrow for cancer cells as well. It is grueling to think about, let alone go through. It's even more disturbing when it involves your 8-year-old son.

We met with several anesthesiologists about his first bone marrow aspiration. As is often the case with a large, urban hospital, everything was delayed. The procedure was supposed to occur at 2 p.m. It was now 5 o'clock. Frankie hadn't consumed anything the entire day. This only added further stress and fatigue to a tense situation. Oddly, our family tends to handle stress with humor. To pass the time, we kept teasing and joking with doctors and nurses. Dressed in his hospital gown the whole day, Frankie was cranky and growing tired. It wasn't like we were waiting online for movie tickets: Frankie was going to have a spinal tap/bone marrow aspiration. No one was enthused about that.

About 5:30 p.m., to break the monotony and shift the dynamics, Keri blurted out: "Let's play 'I Spy'!"

It's a game where one person silently chooses an object in the room. The other players need to guess what that person chose. It starts with a clue: "I spy something that is the color 'X,'" and the other players name objects until guessing the correct one.

We played for a while. Each of us took turns "spying" some silly object in the waiting room for about 30 minutes.

When it was Frankie's turn, I saw his eyes twinkling as they scanned the area for another object. It amazed me that he was this enthusiastic on an empty stomach.

Then it hit me, and the transition occurred. We had spent the first 24 hours of his diagnosis shuffling around, feeling numb and mechanically going through the motions. Robotically, we set up babysitting arrangements and carpooling. We made certain our other two sons got to lacrosse practices, trumpet lessons and play dates. We made sure Frankie was comfortable and adjusting. We did our best to process the reams of information the hospital hurled at us. Yet, sitting in that waiting room, as Frankie excitedly sprang off his seat scanning his surroundings for the next "I Spy" clue, I thought about how beautiful he truly is (and all children are). His innocence, energy, enthusiasm, and sparkle struck me as he played "I Spy" and tried to find some object or color to stump us.

He kept jumping to his feet to answer each question in the game. As he stood in front of me, my awe of him became stark.

I then had a "vision" I'd never experienced before (or since). Sitting in my chair, I "saw" the cancer inside of Frankie. I could see it flowing throughout his body. It was oil black and repulsive. It was moving rapidly. Initially, I was shocked and astonished by it. Then it dawned on me how unforgiving and unrelenting the cancer was. I also grasped that it was aggressively trying to kill him.

Rage surged through me like at no other time in my life. I looked at Frankie, and in my mind I spoke quietly to the cancer.

"Oh my God. Oh my God. There you are. There you are! I see you. Aren't you ruthless and vicious? You're quite cunning and sneaky.

"I know what you are trying to do.

"You're trying to take our boy from us. You want to kill him. You want to kill our little boy. You won't. You will not," I demanded. "We have some of the best doctors in the world right here helping him. We are at one of the best hospitals *in the world*.

You have attacked the wrong child and the wrong family. You want people to fear you, to succumb to you and fail." My eyes started to fill with tears of anger. "You need to know that God has gifted me with an uncommon level of determination to overcome the setbacks in my life. I will unlock every pound of this on you, 'Cancer.' We will destroy you. We will kill you. You do not stand a chance. Let me be very clear, you will not take our boy."

Later that night after Frankie's bone marrow aspiration, one of the doctors advised me that if I was able, it would be better for Frankie to hear the news about the cancer from a parent (and that she would be there to help explain further, if necessary). I needed to tell my son that he had leukemia. I realized, of course, that this was going to be the most difficult conversation I'd ever had. I went to an alcove waiting area on the oncology floor and prayed for guidance. I knew that I needed Frankie's 8-year-old mind to understand. I also needed him to be fearless.

About 10:30 that night, with several doctors and my wife in the room, I sat next to Frank and began.

"So, we have been here at the hospital for a little while already." He nodded. "Do you know why?" I asked.

"I needed some tests done," he answered.

"Frank, you know how the basketball hoop on the trampoline in the yard is broken?"
He nodded.

"So, that needs a new rim...we simply have to buy one and put it up. There are times where things like the trampoline and the Play Station just need to be reset in order to fix them. It's pretty easy."

He nodded again.

"Now, as you know, the go-kart we have in the garage has a broken wheel and the drive chain broke, so it will take more time to get this fixed. At times, people are like things and they get a little sick, and just have to stay home for a while. Other times, they need some more things done on them to get everything back in order, like the go-kart."

Frankie's innocent blue eyes never stopped looking at mine.

"As you know, you weren't feeling well this week, and doctors ran some tests to see what was going on. And, we found out, Frankie, this is going to take some time like it does fixing the go-kart. Unfortunately, Frank, the tests came back and have shown that you have leukemia, which is a form of cancer."

He appeared frightened and confused. And he began to cry.

"I have cancer!!???"

"Yes, Frankie...but we are in one of the best hospitals in the world...with some of the greatest doctors..."

"Am I going to go bald?" he asked.

"Yes, that will probably happen later on…"

He sobbed and sobbed. Keri hugged him. The doctors hugged him. Everyone explained that he was going to defeat this. We reassured him everything was going to be okay and that he was not alone in his fight. He had a team of loving family, friends, nurses, and doctors supporting him. Keri suggested we create a list made up of people he wanted to "draft" to be part of FRANKIE'S TEAM. I then moved away from the bed, sat in a chair in the corner and tried to recover from the most gut-wrenching conversation I'd ever had.

And with that, our war on cancer began…

The Next 72 Hours: "The Sorting Period"

Keri is buoyant, personable and very well loved. She has a throng of friends. As so many friends and family learned about Frankie those first few days, she was besieged with emails, texts and phone calls. In between tending to Frankie, meetings with doctors, spinal procedures and trying to adjust to reality, you could hear her phone buzzing; her email inbox had hundreds of messages. She couldn't respond or reply to any of them.

Finally, a few days after Frankie was diagnosed, she released an email to her network of family and friends on May 31, 2010.

To all our beautiful, loving and giving friends and family...
This is how I truly feel:

EAGLES IN A STORM
Did you know that an eagle knows when a storm is approaching long before it breaks? The eagle will fly to some high spot and wait for the winds to come. When the storm hits, it sets its wings so that the wind will pick it up and lift it above the storm. While the storm rages below, the eagle is soaring above it. The eagle does not escape the storm. It simply uses the storm to lift it higher. It rises on the winds that bring the storm.

When the storms of life come upon us, and all of us will experience them, we can rise above them by setting our minds and our belief toward God. The storms do not have to overcome us. We can allow God's power to lift us above them.

God enables us to ride the winds of the storm that bring sickness, tragedy, failure and disappointment in our lives. We can soar above the storm.

Remember, it is not the burdens of life that weigh us down, it is how we handle them.

But most importantly, this is what I feel our Frankie needs:

Please don't just keep our baby in your prayers. From deep within, scream his name to be heard through the heavens that he maintains his strength and beautiful spirit. So that when we get to the "other side" of this, he's still the same beautiful, *goofy, spirited little boy we've know him to be. Xoxo Keri*

The responses to her post were amazing. Every time you think the world's a bit crazy and you encounter an intense situation, you often see most people's true and kinder sides. So many of the responses lifted our spirits:

Valerie Price
June 1, 2010, 2:28 a.m.
We aren't praying- we are shouting from the rooftops as you had suggested! We are holding clear the KNOWING every day that Frankie is OH SO FINE and this is just part of his continued training to be the superhero of his dreams. There's nothing he can't do and he will show us all to prove the point! Go Frankie! Our hearts are with you all the way as you blaze your path across this frontier, which is no match for your spirit. We love your updates so we can cheer you through and so that your story continues to write across our hearts.
Valerie, Rich and Mackenzie

Karen Warren
June 1, 2010, 2:12 a.m.
Dear Frankie, Keri and family,
We are all with you! Every day, all the time! We think about you, pray for you, and talk about you. The Dezell family ROCKS. Frankie, we miss you in the hallways of PRES [Pound Ridge Elementary School] and can't wait to see you back home! You have a world of support right at home; you are a hero - an ordinary individual who finds the strength to persevere and endure in spite of overwhelming obstacles.-- (Christopher Reeve) xoxo Karen, Alan, Seneca and Susha Warren.

Jennifer Santulli
June 1, 2010, 11:35 p.m.
Dear Frankie,
We are all praying for you to have a quick recovery! You are sooo brave, Frankie! I know your mom and dad are taking great care of you. You and your family are very special to us all.
With all our love and support,
The Santulli Family

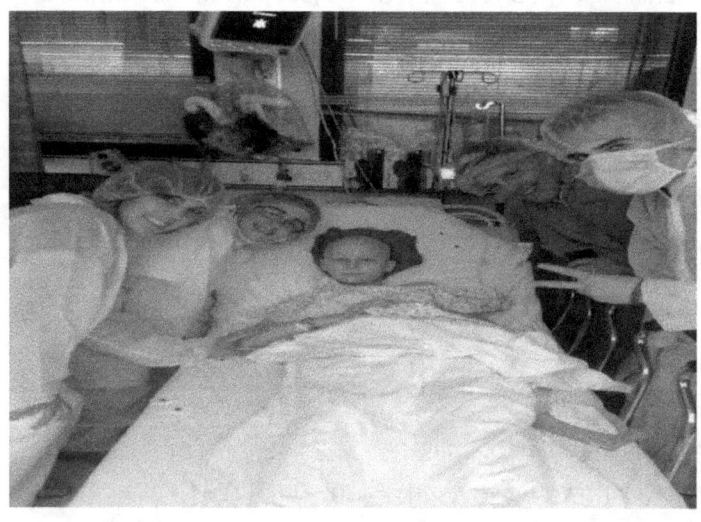

May 2010: We *made the decision very early that our whole family was "all in" on Frankie's fight.*

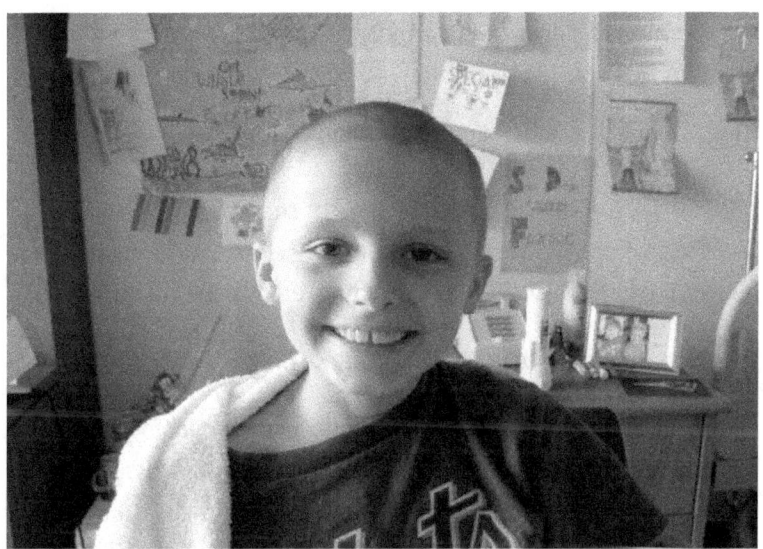

By mid-June, our main man's head was shaved, and he was ready for the fight.

Understanding the Cancer Beast: "A Layman's Perspective"

Very early on in the treatment protocol, I tried to gain a better grasp of what cancer actually is, and what specifically leukemia does. Frankie was diagnosed with acute lymphoblastic leukemia, or ALL. I am a reasonably intelligent man, but my background is in finance and sales. So, when I heard all the doctors talking about "red blood cells," "white blood cells," "platelets" and the like, I had no idea how to make sense of it all. I kept reading about leukemia and trying to understand how and why it occurs.

I came up with a simple analogy that relates to the corporate world. One night, I sat down with a couple of his doctors and ran it by them.

"Okay, you two," I began. "I am trying to understand leukemia a bit better, and because I'm a moron I have to frame the whole thing more around my own environment and experiences."

The two doctors looked at one another and nodded.

"So, I work for a large company, and at this company we have a lot of copying machines. You often advise me that the white blood/cancer cells in Frankie's body overtook the healthy cells?"

The doctors nodded again.

"So, if I have this right, *the body* is like a copy machine. You put what you want to copy in the copy machine, you press the number of copies you want and the machine makes that number of copies. These copies look like...well, copies of the original. Occasionally, something goes amiss with a copier and it starts to produce bad copies, copies that don't look like the original. AND, instead of making the number of copies you want, it just keeps making more and more bad copies.

"So, if I have this right, *cancer* is also like a copy machine. Cancer causes a few bad cells or copies to be made and instead of the body rejecting those bad cells, more and more unhealthy cells then get replicated or copied. To the point that the body—or the copy machine—just keeps making flawed copies or cells?"

The doctors didn't nod at this point but did affirm my analogy.

"And what we're going to try to do with all the chemotherapy is to destroy all the bad copies and actually re-train the body to only produce healthy cells going forward?"

Again, the doctors didn't give a thorough medical stamp of approval, but they sort of agreed with my comparison.

From witnessing other people who have been stricken with cancer, I have seen how harsh the treatments can be. When it's suddenly your child going through hell, it's even more shocking. We realized early on that treating cancer is horrible to endure and distressing to witness. You understand immediately that the disease is deadly. You also learn that after all the centuries that cancer has been around, the only way to control it is by essentially poisoning it. The chemotherapy, radiation or other methods of treatment are fundamentally venom. And you're taking the patient's body to the brink of death. As is common, cancer patients typically lose their hair. The nausea and vomiting are brutal. The body is stripped of all its regular defenses, so other illnesses can easily creep in and cause more issues. At some point, a patient is so depleted by the assault, no further medicine can be given until the body regroups and the healthy blood cell "counts" rise.

The periods between Frankie's treatments were horrible. His immune system was so weakened by the chemo and medication he would frequently have fevers from the infections. The nausea was violent. The hair loss was troubling. The bloating from all the steroids he was taking was disturbing. Meanwhile, the pain in his bones was acute and his muscles were weakened, making it difficult for him to walk even just a few steps.

The speed of Frankie's transformation was stunning: In early May 2010, Frankie was a scrappy and wiry little lacrosse player weighing 60 pounds. By mid-June, he had lost 9 pounds, was bald, gaunt, moon-faced by steroids, and had dark circles under his eyes.

Besides living with the medications and their ruthless side

effects, Frankie's psyche was suffering, too. One night, he awoke sweating and panicked, yelling out, "What is happening to me?" He was in a cold sweat. He was hyperventilating. "What is happening to me!?!"

I hugged him and gave him a kiss. I explained that he was sick…that he was going to get better…and that we were going to make sure of this.

At another point early in the treatments, Frankie had been hammered all day with chemo, prednisone (steroids) and various other drugs. I stayed with him that night at the hospital, and he woke up around 3 a.m. needing to urinate. The doctors wanted him to void into a container so they could test the sample to track his kidney functions/output. He was quite groggy and walked unsteadily toward the lavatory in his room. All his IV lines were attached to a pole. I called out to remind him that he needed to pee in the container.

I rose from the futon, grabbed the urinal bottle and knelt in front of him. He was so tired and dazed. His IV line then got caught on the end of the bed. He lost control of his direction and urinated all over my head. Not wanting to upset him, I remained quiet and then positioned his arms and hands so he could finish in the container. After helping him back into bed, I scampered off to the hospital bathroom and took the longest shower of my life.

The next morning when the doctors made their rounds, I quietly told them what had happened. They looked alarmed and sat me in a chair. A pair of doctors from the Infectious Disease Department were called.

"The urine hit your eyes," one of them said, poking a flashlight toward my face.

"Yes," I replied.

"Well, that's dangerous! His urine contains active chemo from yesterday's treatments and that can do damage to your cornea."

I assured them I was okay and that I had thoroughly washed afterward. As the doctors left the room, I thought: *So, Frankie's urine can burn my eyes because of the chemotherapy. How disturbing is it that the same crap is being dumped into his body to thwart the cancer?*

The Next 100 Days: "Making Miracles & Magic within Mayhem"

In the first few weeks after Frankie's diagnosis, we quickly realized that the life we had known was over. Frank's treatments were agonizing. It was harrowing to watch your child endure it. We were within an orbit of ugliness that none of us knew what to do with. It is then that we started to be spiritually guided in how to navigate this. We decided that fueling life (and not cancer) was the only path. Our family energy became "crazier than cancer." The action, support and love we received from around the world became our petroleum.

Keri and I took turns spending the night sleeping on the futon in Frankie's hospital room. Each day and evening, chemo, steroids, painkillers and other medicines were delivered intravenously. Each night, as the IVs and medications concluded, alarms would sound. If we were lucky, we'd average about 2.5 hours of uninterrupted sleep before the next alarm would go off. It was not a restful period.

Frankie's classmates, friends from religious study, neighbors, teachers and others made artwork, get-well cards and drawings for him. Keri diligently hung each item in his room. Her focus was to surround him with every element of positivity to fend off the cancer. His surroundings looked like a party store.

Meanwhile, flickers of life's goodness were being woven into our bubble. Word of Frankie's illness literally went global. I was astonished by how decent and kind so many strangers were. A friend from Italy arranged to have daily Masses celebrated for him in the predominantly Catholic country. A group of nuns prayed for him in Ireland. In one of the most poignant episodes, a group in Haiti (a country that had experienced a devastating earthquake earlier that year) prayed for him via another friend's connections to an international prayer chain.

We kept receiving emails and notes from people we had never met. Amidst the chaos of our lives, I was deeply touched by the outpouring of support and the goodness in so many people's hearts:

Hello. My name is Jenna. I live in New Hope, Penn. (near Philadelphia), and I am a good friend of Shelly's cousin Mike. When this email was sent to me, I have to tell you, I was so inspired. I think that this is an amazing thing to do for your Frankie, and I am so honored to be a part of it. I work with children, and there is nothing more heartbreaking to me than to see a child in pain...I have also forwarded this to about 50 of my

friends and family from all over the country, so be looking for many more emails and prayers in the coming days!
Much Love,
Jenna

Keri established a CaringBridge webpage/blog to provide updates on Frankie's progress. It was healing for her to write, to witness the support around Frankie, and to interact.

The numerous responses to her blog were touching and sometimes written directly to Frankie. Many were from strangers. I kept wondering why people from all over the world who didn't even know Frankie would take the time to write to him. I found it remarkable and it helped center me.

Hi, My name is Mike and I am writing from Appleton, Wisconsin (if you look on a map you will see it's about 30 miles south of Green Bay). My friend Kevin has told me you got a little bit of bad news lately. I wanted to send you an email and let you know that I'll be thinking of you and saying some prayers for you. I have no doubt in my mind that you are going to be fine since you are young and very strong. I am originally from Minneapolis and I am a big Twins fan (the Twins can't seem to beat the Yankees can they?). I hear you are a really good baseball player and I bet you can be as good as my favorite players Joe Mauer and Justin Morneau. Take care Frankie,
Mike

Hi, You don't know us but we received an email asking for prayers for Frankie. My name is AnnMarie and I live in Connecticut. My daughter was treated for ALL (diagnosed in May

2007) and finished in August 2009. I would be very happy to talk to you if you would like the personal and empathetic support of someone who understands. I also have a friend in Ridgefield whose 2-year-old is currently in treatment for ALL and she has offered her support as well.... I will be praying for Frankie. Keep your faith in God strong and remember that nothing that happens in your day escapes His awareness. He hears your prayers and heaven will be stormed with requests for Frankie's healing...and the Lord will hear and answer. His is a mighty and wonderful God. Build your faith stronger day by day. Matthew 7:7...ask and you shall receive, seek and you shall find, knock and it shall be opened to you. I prayed that verse everyday...and still do. May God bless you with his healing. God be with you.
AnnMarie

One of Keri's dear friends, Marisa, started a prayer chain on Frankie's behalf. She asked that a person from each state pray for Frankie. The friend's note soliciting prayers will forever be etched in my mind:

Let each of us pray daily for Frankie and his family and let us reach out to our own family and friends from all over the USA and ask for prayers. Soon each state in the USA will be praying for the Dezells. Please ask your family and friends to send me a brief email...from the state they represent and I will tell Keri and Jim to mark it on the map. I am also printing out all the emails I receive and making a book of prayers called "Frankie's Angels," so feel free to email me with your prayers!

She made a map of the United States and presented it to Keri.

We marked off each state where there was at least one person committed to praying for Frankie. It was amazing, and Keri displayed it in his room.

About three weeks into his treatment regimen, Frankie and I were hanging out in his room and he was pale from all the medication. He had about five IV lines attached to his pole. God only knows what kind of cancer-fighting therapy was getting dumped into him that day. After he had used the restroom and I was helping him back into bed, Frankie accidentally pulled the wheels of the IV pole over my toe. I grimaced (IV poles are heavy), and Frankie was apologetic. I jokingly told him that if he ever did that again, I'd have no other option but to beat him to a pulp. He replied, "I'd like to see you try."

I saw him standing there in his pajamas, all gray, gaunt and bald. But in his eyes, I just saw that flicker, that twinkle of mischievousness that had always been there. He wanted to play.

Before I describe what happened next, I must explain something. In a home with three boys (four when you include me), we did a great deal of roughhousing and wrestling. As Frankie and I stood there staring at each other that night, I realized all he wanted amidst all the IVs and medicine was to have some fun. So, I reached down, grabbed the ends of the pillow from my bed and hit him with it. Quite hard. I didn't do it gently since he'd know I was holding back because he was "sick." I wanted him to forget about that for a moment, remember that he was still my son, and that we could still roughhouse.

After I whacked him with the pillow, he (and his IV pole) fell backward onto the bed. He sprang back up, pulled up his pillow and swung it at me. For anyone who decides to engage in a pillow fight with someone connected to an intravenous pole in a hospital room, I have some advice: You, as the assailant, hold a significant advantage. The patients can move only as far as their IV lines allow. In addition, they are not able to turn quickly, so it is easy to get behind them and attack.

I was knocking Frankie to Kingdom Come. Each time he'd swing at me, he was limited by the IV lines. He would swing, miss, and then I would pummel him.

We were having a blast. He was laughing and yelling. Everything was great. Then, one of the more rigid nurses came into the room.

"Is everything okay in here?" she asked.

"No...my dad is pummeling me with pillows" Frankie laughingly replied. The nurse was alarmed and a bit concerned. "It's okay," Frankie assured her. "I am fine."

The nurse looked at me sternly and then cautiously left the room.

I turned to Frankie and said, "You ratted on me, you little turd."

I pushed Frankie down on the bed. I then took two pillows, covered his face with them and began to hit them repeatedly. I could hear his muffled laughter and giddy screaming. I kept playfully yelling at him and accusing him of being a snitch. I then sat up, pulled the pillows from his face and saw something magnificent: He was laughing and smiling, and his eyes were twinkling. This delighted me. I realized that the more insanity we added to this ride, the more we normalized it. The more thrills we added to each day, the more manageable we made it.

One night a few days later, Frankie was stable and felt good. He sent me out to get him some spareribs from a Chinese takeout place nearby. As the result of steroids, cancer patients often get insatiable cravings for various foods.

As I returned to his hospital room, a female coworker who had been away for a month called me on my mobile phone. She had met Frankie in April when it was "Bring Your Kids to Work Day" and truly enjoyed him. She was distraught over Frankie being sick and was choked up. Frankie's nurse, Andy, was in the room. Andy worked at night and had a rapport with him. He loved her, and he would often speak with her when she began her shift at 7 p.m.

"I can't believe he's sick," the coworker said. "When you brought him into the office, he was so charming and energetic."

The coworker went on to praise Frankie and apologized for not being able to get in touch sooner. As she spoke, I watched Frankie in his bed. He was thoroughly enjoying the attention from Andy and was giggling. Andy started to leave and mentioned to Frankie in a whisper: "If you need anything, you know what to do...just buzz me, and I'll be right over."

Frankie smiled, confirmed that he knew what to do by holding up the clicker with the nurse's buzzer, and watched her leave. My admiration and respect for nurses had surged throughout Frankie's ordeal: They often are some of the most compassionate and patient people you will ever meet.

After Andy's departure, Frankie used the clicker to adjust his bed and turn on the TV. He pulled over his tray table and began chowing down on the Chinese food.

Meanwhile, my coworker continued to sob. "So, can I ask...how is Frankie doing right now? Is he doing okay?"

I looked at him, comfortable in his bed, clicker in hand, gnawing on a Chinese rib and watching a show.

"How is he? You want to know how Frankie is?" I repeated to my coworker.

"Actually...he's not doing too badly today."

"Really?" she asked.

"Yes," I replied. "Right now, he's sitting up in his bed...inhaling Chinese food...watching *SpongeBob SquarePants* on TV...and all he has to do is press a button—and a beautiful woman shows up and will give him whatever he wants."

My colleague burst out laughing.

"It's like every guy's dream," I explained.

The next weekend, hospital staff gave us a pass to leave for one night and go out as a family. We booked a hotel room in lower Manhattan and rolled there to do something different and fun.

Frankie's immune system was still quite compromised, so Keri took an arsenal of disinfectants, towelettes and wipes to clean the hotel room before he entered.

Frank wanted to see a movie, but not before Keri disinfected the theater area and covered our seats with sheets to avoid any germs. We were lucky that we chose to see a matinee because it was a beautiful summer day and the theater was empty. This made for a perfect setup for our immunocompromised little boy. We saw *Toy Story 3* and the remake of *The Karate Kid*.

Afterward, several of his cousins and an aunt and uncle from Boston arrived to visit with him. We hung out in Battery Park and played catch with a football. Frankie was thrilled and enjoyed himself tremendously. After being in the hospital for more than four weeks, it was nice for him to get outside.

A few days later, we returned to the hospital to begin the next phase of Frankie's treatment. Frank's doctors met privately with Keri and me. They informed us that they had come across an oddity in his form of cancer. Frankie was originally diagnosed with ALL (acute lymphoblastic leukemia). Doctors also noticed that he had the markings for another form of cancer called Burkitt's leukemia. They explained that this was going to change his treatment regimen, putting him through cycles that were going to be far more aggressive and brutal than the ALL plan. There was one positive outcome: Because the treatments would be more intense, they would conclude in 2.5 years instead of the 3 years it typically takes when treating ALL. The doctors said that ALL with the markings for Burkitt's was a rare cancer to find in adults, and even rarer in children.

Keri and I listened intently. Although the rarity was concerning, we chose not to focus on that. While we did not like that the treatments would be more severe, we were grateful for the reduced treatment schedule. We continued switching nights at the hospital, which we had been doing for more than a month. We stayed in one room, and Keri or I would sleep on the futon. Frankie would sometimes join us because the hospital bed reminded him that he was sick. With so many IV alarms going off each night, and the futon not the most comfortable bed, it certainly wasn't the ideal arrangement. But we were glad we could be with him, and in the same room.

Shortly after they told us about the Burkitt's markings, doctors and nurses indicated that they might send Frankie home for a few days while his body recovered from the chemo. The treatment had taken his white blood cell "count"—the level of white blood cells in his body—so low that any further chemo would do severe harm (meaning death or risk of extreme infections).

Frankie overheard the chatter about his brief release and was overjoyed. He asked when he was getting out and was told probably the next day. Then, one of the doctors came in with some sobering news.

"Frankie," she said. "We'd love to discharge you, and we can tell how much you want to go."

Frankie's bald head nodded furiously.

"However, we did some bloodwork this morning, and there's unfortunately a real deficiency in your potassium levels. Until those numbers go up, we cannot let you go."

Frankie's eyes pooled with tears.

"How can I get my potassium level up?" he asked desperately.

"Well," she replied, "a natural way is for you to eat more food with high potassium…"

"Like what?" Frankie interrupted. "What food do I need to eat?"

"Potatoes, avocados, bananas…," the doctor advised.

"Dad, go get me some fucking bananas!" Frankie instructed (I'll address his swearing a bit later).

I left the room to run to the local supermarket, and Keri stayed to hear what else the doctor had to say.

While I was in line at the grocery store, it occurred to me that Frankie actually hated bananas. Nevertheless, I brought them to his room and he started CRAMMING the fruit into his mouth. Keri also found a potassium supplement that he could take. Before the day was over, the little lunatic had inhaled two bunches of bananas and taken all the supplements. He was so focused on getting out of the hospital, he didn't care. He would push bananas through his ears if that gave him enough potassium to escape confinement.

The next day doctors performed a Complete Blood Test (checking white/red/platelet cell counts) and an Electrolyte panel (a blood test that checks electrolytes including potassium) again, and Frankie's potassium levels were high enough for his release. The timing was perfect: It was Father's Day weekend. The discharge process began at 10 a.m., but by the time all the paperwork was finalized it was 3:30 p.m. No matter to Frankie; he was ecstatic.

By this stage, Frankie had been in the hospital for over a month.

While our family was working hard to do everything we could for Frankie and to make best of the situation, a startling trend infected everyone in our immediate family: We could not stop <u>swearing</u>.

Before cancer's arrival in our lives, we had always been rather controlled, guarded and good about muzzling our foul language. Yet, that first month, while we held it together remarkably well on many fronts, all hell broke loose with our cursing. During the first 30 days, cancer had brought our family closer. We were tougher from it. We were definitely more jaded but, at the same time, more cohesive.

The swearing started with innocent blurts and outcries. But as the insanity of cancer flooded our lives, profanity became habit-forming. So much so that 10-year-old Max—disturbed by the frequency of the vulgar language being exchanged—created a "<u>No Cursing Treaty</u>." Each of us signed it and agreed that we were allowed to curse only when:

- A. We were telling a joke.
- B. We hurt ourselves accidentally.
- C. We were talking about something related to cancer.

Max proudly hung the signed pact on our kitchen wall as a reminder. The treaty remained there for the next six years. It was effective, in reality, for only seven days.

As we were preparing to leave the hospital on the day of his brief liberation, Frankie asked for permission to make obscene gestures at cancer and the hospital as we drove away. We gave him "authorization" because, as the treaty clearly defined, it was cancer related. So, as we pulled away from the valet parking area, with Frankie popping up through the sunroof, he made every obscene gesture he knew how. It was quite a sight to see this bald 8-year-old spewing expletives and giving the middle finger to anything and everything as we drove down 165th Street.

Back home, we treated Frankie to one of his favorite meals and made s'mores in the backyard fire pit. We played football and basketball, and allowed some friends, who wore surgical masks, to visit. It was a unique Father's Day, to say the least.

Amidst the joy of having Frank home for a few days, the realities and burden of cancer quickly displayed themselves.

Because the body is flooded with chemo drugs, the patient's blood cell "counts" drop, which can lead to infections. These infections typically become evident in the form of fevers. If Frankie's fever escalated, he had to be readmitted to the hospital.

According to hospital protocol, if his fever climbed above 100.3 (which is quite common for cancer patients), we needed to drive Frankie 40 miles back to the hospital in Manhattan and check him in through the emergency room. The ER physicians would then decide whether to admit him or send him to the pediatric oncology ward.

For whatever reason, most of Frankie's fevers occurred at night. And the thought of bringing an 8-year-old to a New York City emergency room in the midnight hour was a bit disquieting. A few days after the Father's Day festivities, Frankie developed a fever over the threshold. So, off to the hospital we went at 11 p.m. Upon our arrival, we saw that the ER was full. Heroin addicts and people with gunshot wounds were being treated in hallways. Because Frankie had a compromised immune system, he was swiftly ushered into an isolated room donning a surgical mask. It was all quite bizarre.

At one point that night, Frankie overheard a nurse inform her colleagues that "Frankie didn't belong in the emergency room" and that he should soon be transferred to 5 Tower (the pediatric oncology section of the hospital). The nurse then said she used to work in 5 Tower, but she left that job because it was known as the "Death Tower."

Frankie was shaken to his core. It was the only negative encounter we ever had with any medical personnel. The nurse was later reprimanded.

The ER doctors evaluated Frankie and decided to admit him to the oncology floor. Keri stayed with him that night, and I drove home to be with Max and James. Frankie could not shake off what he heard that nurse say. He was still rattled by it a few hours later. It prompted him to ask Keri and his oncology nurse, Paige, whether he was going to die. It was terrible. Keri and Paige did everything they could to console him.

The next day, Keri called me to give an update on what Frankie had overheard and how it had played out. It was now my turn to spend the night.

"Be prepared because our little friend will probably be asking the same question," Keri warned.

As I drove to the hospital, I thought about how I never imagined I would have to field that question from my child. I decided to wait until Keri left before I broached the subject with Frankie. Then I pulled my chair over to the side of his bed.

"So, you heard what that nurse said last night, right?" I asked.

He nodded his steroid-bloated head.

"I am sorry she said something like that, Frank, and I am very sorry you had to hear it."

I put my face closer to his and prayed for God's guidance.

"You want to know if you are going to die? No, Frank, you are not going to die," I implored. "And do you want to know why?"

I got off the chair, knelt on one knee and looked into his eyes.

"You are not going to die, Frank, for three reasons," I said.

"Number one, you are being treated at Columbia University, which is one of the greatest hospitals in the world. This is where your grandmother [nicknamed Bamma] went to school, Frank, and if you don't think she had some influence over this from heaven—she did. Bamma is watching over you from heaven.

"Secondly, you know your mom is one of the most loving people in the world. She has people all over the globe praying for you, Frankie. There are nuns in Ireland...people in Haiti...churches in Italy...and people all around the United States praying for you."

Frank glanced at the floor and then looked back at me. I could tell he wanted to know how I, specifically, was engaged in all of this.

"And the last thing that I need to tell you, Frank, is that I am not as loving or as compassionate as your mom. I don't have a lot of friends or prayer networks all over the place. But what God did give me, Frank, is an uncommon level of determination to overcome the things that I have needed to overcome in life. And I pray each night to God that this same determination gets instilled in you for you to destroy this."

Frankie beamed at me. I hugged him and kissed his bald head.

As I got up, I decided that we needed to change the mood and energy of this death talk. I did not want him to be afraid at all. I wanted him to understand that this was a fight—and that while it was going to be grueling at times, he was going to win.

Then, an idea flashed into my brain.

"Frankie, what do you think your two brothers are doing at the house right now?"

"I don't know…probably hanging out with mom and watching TV," he replied.

"What do you think they're watching?"

"Probably *SpongeBob* or *iCarly*."

"Frankie, do you think either of your brothers has ever seen a movie that was rated R?"

Frankie looked at me a bit puzzled, but curious.

"No…I don't think so…"

"So, Frank, your brothers are home, bored, doing homework, eating dinner and then watching television, right?"

He nodded quizzically.

"You and I are here. It's just the two of us. We have this iPad that my coworkers got you. Let's you and me watch an R-rated movie."

Frankie was instantaneously sold.

"But here's the deal, Frank. You <u>cannot</u> ever tell anyone we did this because you are only 8 years old. You shouldn't be watching R-rated movies, and I could get into a lot of trouble for this…"

Frankie was enthralled. He sprang off the bed.

"Which one?" His eyes sparkled. "What R-rated movie?"

I whispered to him. "It is a movie called *Gladiator*, Frankie. It's about a warrior, just like you."

So, we downloaded the movie and watched it together, lying on the futon.

During one scene, Maximus (played by Russell Crowe) decapitates another gladiator in the arena. Frankie stood up in astonishment.

"Did he just chop his head off?" he asked. "Oh my God, Dad, did he just cut his head off?"

"Yep!" I replied, smiling. "He just took his head off. And you want to know something, Frankie?"

His puffy steroid face turned to me.

"This is exactly what you are going to do to cancer."

One week after clandestinely watching the movie, everyone in our town mysteriously knew my youngest son had seen an R-rated film!?! So much for an 8-year-old keeping his end of a promise.

We were blessed: The country (and the world, for that matter) was praying for Frankie.

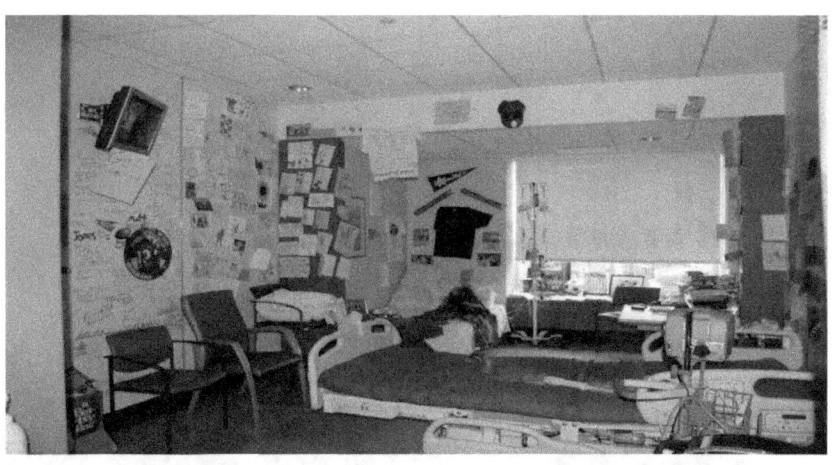

Keri turned Frankie's room into a festival of positive vibes and healing energy. Photos, love notes and well-wishes eventually covered every inch of his hospital room walls.

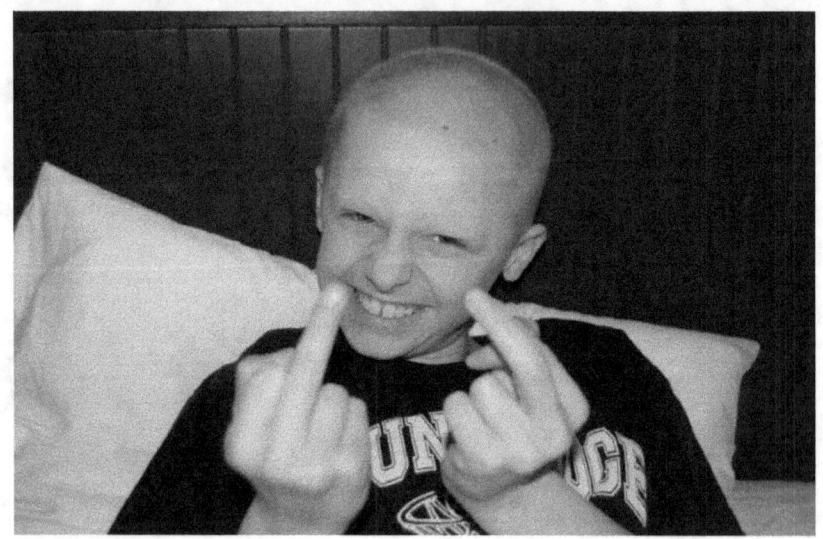

Frankie's personal message to cancer. Our "No Cursing Treaty" lasted only days.

Frankie's unconventional farewell wave to the hospital when doctors let him out after 45 days.

An Unusual Request from the 8-Year Old Gladiator

The spring of 2010 slowly inched forward, and we kept rattling along in our new life. Max and James were in the final weeks of school before summer break, and Frankie's chemo treatments marched on. During this phase, when Frankie's blood cell counts would drop, he'd come home to regain his strength, with the agreement that we would bring him daily to Columbia University's clinic in Manhattan for outpatient visits.

Once his body had recovered, he would be readmitted to the hospital for another seven or so days and repeat the cycle. The unusual combination of ALL and Burkitt's leukemia necessitated an individualized treatment plan specific to Frankie. The regimen was extremely aggressive.

In one particular week, Frankie underwent three—yes, *three*—separate spinal taps. Under anesthesia, Frankie endured the withdrawal of spinal fluid to check for cancer cells and then received an injection of chemotherapy—with an 8-inch needle—into his spine.

The combination of his not being able to eat or drink for eight hours before the anesthesia, the process of administering the medicine, and the nausea that occurred afterward—it was always a disaster. Throughout this phase, Frankie looked scrawny and gaunt. He resembled young cast members of *The Walking Dead*. Another set of tests required that he drink barium fluid—a liquid used to identify areas of concern more easily during body scans. He would vomit each time he drank it, so he began refusing it. On one occasion, we spent hours with doctors and nurses trying to coerce him to consume it. I would drink some of the barium fluid, too, just to commiserate with him. Even this didn't work after a while. He simply refused. We reached exhaustion in the negotiations. I finally told him that if he would finish the drink, he would be permitted to leave the hospital for a few days in between his treatments. I also tempted him by saying I'd do whatever he wanted once we got home. He perked up at the thought.

"Anything?" he asked slyly.

The nurses were still in the room, trying to encourage him to finish the barium.

"Yes, anything, Frank," I replied with a sigh.

He pondered the offer a few more seconds and then leaned forward.

"When we get out of the hospital...," he whispered.

"Yes," I replied.

"You and I are going to play football."

"Okay," I agreed.

Our whole family loves football, so I wasn't surprised by the request.

Frankie then started to laugh. "But not just any kind of football...".

"Okay, then, what kind of football are we going to play?"

He whispered in my ear.

"We're going to play...we are going to play...*naked* football!"

"The only way that I am going to finish that shitty drink is if you play NAKED football with me when we get out of here."

With my head cocked back, I looked at him, startled. He was laughing and nodding his head.

Well, I thought, what the hell.

"Okay," I repeated. "You're on. I'll play naked football with you. But only if you finish that stuff."

He gulped it down, and the next day he was released from the hospital for a few days.

It always felt like we were making a prison break each time we left the building. We were joyous.

The first night we were home, as I was helping to clear the dinner dishes, a voice summoned me outside. I looked in our back yard and saw Frank's haggard body wearing nothing, but a smile and he was grasping a football.

"Come on, Dad, you promised," he gleefully demanded.

I could only laugh.

Out I went, a naked fool, throwing and catching a football with him and his brother Max, who stripped down to join us. James was at a CYO basketball practice, so he managed to escape the evening shenanigans. Frankie was laughing hysterically. It was magical.

As promised, we returned to the clinic the next day. The nurses were preparing to administer a chemo IV into Frankie's arm. One of them, who had been tipped off to the grand bargain night before, grinned and asked, "So, Frankie, how was that football game last night? Was there anything unique about it?"

It certainly wasn't the Father's Day I had expected in 2010, but we made the best of it.

The infamous "Naked Bowl," with Max also baring all to get in the game. I now truly understood the saying that parents will do anything for their kids.

Managing the Other Two Brothers

In our efforts to find segments and swatches of sanity during the mayhem of cancer, Frankie's cravings for food kept us busy. He was on a lot of steroids, and this resulted in his insatiable appetite. Some mornings we'd get him a sausage, egg and cheese bagel sandwich from a shop seven blocks away. No sooner had you returned with that, he'd have a lunch menu in hand, rattling off what he wanted after he finished the bagel sandwich.

With so much attention required on Frankie, Keri and I were also extremely conscious of his two brothers. We wanted their lives to be as normal and disruption-free as possible. Our family members were great and came in from around the country to assist. Still, James and Max wanted BOTH of their parents around, too. We later learned that James was shouldering many things on his own because he didn't want to give us anything else to worry about. Incredibly thoughtful and admirable of him but upsetting that we were unaware of it.

Keri would help them with homework, provide dinnertime visits and keep them organized. I continued to coach James in lacrosse and tried to be around as much as possible. Our situation was never ideal or perfect, but we were mindful of their needs and did the best we could.

One night I was at the hospital with Frankie. Keri was at home putting Max, 10, to bed, and she noticed he was rather solemn. When she asked what was wrong, he burst into tears.

"I miss Dad!!!" he blurted out. "I need...to see...to be with...Dad."

Keri shared this interaction that night, and we figured out a way for Max to have a "date" with me. I took a day off from work and committed myself fully to him. I dropped him off at school and picked him up early for a doctor's appointment. Then we went out to dinner. As we waited for our food, I asked him: "So, Mom tells me that you want to talk with me?"

Max nodded.

"So, I am sorry that I haven't been around a lot due to Frankie's treatments. But tonight, I am all yours. You've got me 'one on one.' What do you want to talk about?"

Max, a creative and rather proper little fellow, was grateful that we had this time together. He pushed up his glasses, put his napkin on his lap and began to speak.

"So, Dad, I was just wondering…"

I was at the edge of my seat.

"I just wanted to know…"

"Yes, Max."

"If Superman and Batman were to get into a fight, who do you think would win?"

Though I was puzzled, I didn't miss a beat.

"Superman," I responded. "Hands down."

"Why do you say that?"

"Because the only thing that can kill Superman is kryptonite, and

Batman can get killed by a lot of different items."

"Who do you think would win a fight, Superman versus The Hulk?" he then asked.

We sat there for two hours, and I fielded similar questions. We discussed every possible superhero fight imaginable. Once we ran out of superheroes, we focused on which dog breeds would win fights with other animals.

We then got ice cream after dinner. As I tucked Max into bed, I asked if he enjoyed the evening. He nodded and smiled.

Mission accomplished.

Little League Honors, Fireworks & Incredible Neighbors

When the school year ended in late June (one month after diagnosis), our world was riddled with Frankie's bone marrow aspirations, steroids, chemo and hospital stays. As harrowing as all of this was, simple, beautiful gestures and outreaches kept coming our way. They really made a difference in how we were able to manage our efforts.

The Little League team in our town had won a championship. Marking the occasion, one of the coaches wrote on Keri's blog:

Hey, Frankie. It's Dan (Vincent's dad). I want you to know we are all rooting for you and can't wait to see you on the baseball field. I'm not sure if you know but this Saturday is the minors' championship game and our team (the Phillies) and the Blue Jays will be playing each other. This game will be played in honor of you with every one of us wearing those really cool "Team Frankie" green wristbands. So know, that on Saturday at 1:00, you'll have hundreds of Bedford and Pound Ridge fans, parents and players sending their well wishes and prayers to you.

The church and prayer services being offered for Frankie continued around the world and the ongoing outreach from strangers were other remarkable displays of human decency.

Additionally, one of Keri's friends created an interactive calendar for volunteers to sign up to prepare and deliver meals to us several days a week (the MealTrain website didn't exist then). Three or four times a week, delicious meals were delivered to a cooler in our driveway. Neither Keri nor I had to cook on weekdays. We often didn't even know the people who prepared or delivered the food. This went on for over two years!

At one point, my unmarried brother, Tom, had visited to watch Max and James while Keri and I were at the hospital. As a single man, he was accustomed to his routine and eating a lot of fast food. One night, I arrived home to discover the boys and him eating homemade lasagna and bragging about how delicious the steak tips were from the night before. For my brother, accustomed to eating at Applebee's and Five Guys, the "duty" of watching James and Max was like he had died and gone to heaven. Delicious and comforting meals delivered to the house each night—Tom thought he had won the lottery and was living like a king.

It was heartwarming to see this touching side of life because the next phase of treatment was ferocious. As expected, Frankie developed a fever during a treatment break at home and once again was readmitted to Columbia University's Morgan Stanley

Children's Hospital around Independence Day.

Each Fourth of July, our town has an annual road race. Without our knowledge, our friend established a "TEAM FRANKIE" in his honor and participants ran the 5-kilometer race with green Team Frankie T-shirts, reflecting his favorite color. We were extremely touched.

The evening of July Fourth, we were saddened because Frankie was hospitalized and couldn't attend the town's fireworks show. Fortunately, New York City officials had decided to launch fireworks that night from the West Side's Hudson River (not on the usual location of the East River)—giving Frankie a direct view of the pyrotechnics. James, Max and I (with a surprise visit from Frankie's Aunt Erin and cousin Joe) joined Keri and Frank at the hospital. We ordered in some takeout food and got Frankie situated in a tall chair by the window.

About 9:15 p.m., our seemingly private show began. We turned off all the lights in the room to reduce glare, and Keri and I sat behind the boys as their faces pressed against the glass. It was a magnificent sight: The silhouette of Frankie's bald head with protruding ears and his enthralled expression as he enjoyed the celebration.

A week later, Frank returned home for a few days. Then we'd boomerang him back to the hospital for another cycle of chemo that was stronger than before. The respite in between this madness kept us going, as we tried harder to keep our outlook as upbeat, positive and crazy as possible.

Amber alert: "There's a kidnapped leukemia patient"

My mother had owned a summer house since 1976 on Cape Cod

and left it to my four siblings and me in 2006. Our family had grown to love it so much over the years that it became embedded in our DNA and provided an annual vacation spot.

Frankie would tell nurses about his favorite ice cream shop there and describe the beaches. The house is not fancy, but it rests on a peaceful and laid-back part of the Cape. Throughout the summer, I secretly explored ways to see if we could take Frankie and his brothers there, even for a day. I knew that it would be beneficial for all of us to have just a bit of normalcy in a bucolic setting. Keri learned I was looking into the possibility and put a kibosh on the entire concept. She said there was no way it was going to happen. Undeterred, I kept searching for solutions. I'd often talk with the doctors in "code," using only the Cape Cod ZIP Code, 02659, to determine the likelihood. The doctors thought I was out of my mind. But, I would bring up my plan often.

"Look, I know it is 250 miles away from here. However, as smart as all of you are at Columbia, I know that certain guidance that you've gotten on Frankie's leukemia is from the Dana-Farber Cancer Institute in Boston. When we are on Cape Cod, we may be 250 miles from here, but we are only 80 miles from Dana-Farber. It's not like we're in the back woods of Newfoundland."

The doctors would usually just chuckle and say "no" because the timing wasn't right with Frankie's regimen. Nevertheless, I kept monitoring how many days it took his body to recover in between treatments: The time frame was getting more protracted because his body was so ravaged and stripped of defenses.

In late August 2010, Frankie was scheduled to be readmitted. However, his body was so hammered and depleted by the latest round of treatment he was not ready for more chemo. I figured this could be the perfect opportunity to kidnap the little bald kid and take him to Cape Cod. Understanding that I was going to encounter massive resistance from my wife, doctors and nurses, I was preemptive and called the paramedics and EMT squad on Cape Cod.

"Chatham EMT, how can we help you?"

"Hi, my name is Jim Dezell and my family has owned a home in South Chatham for 35 years. I need you to sit tight because I have a very unusual thing to bounce by you, and I need your feedback."

I filled him in on Frankie's story and about wanting to abscond with him to the Cape. I explained that if my plan worked and Frankie required medical assistance, I'd need the Chatham first responders to transport him to Dana-Farber, the premiere pediatric cancer center, in less than 60 minutes. After I finished detailing my plot, there was silence on the other end of the phone. Finally, the paramedic spoke.

"So, let me make sure I have this right. You want me to assure you that Chatham first responders can get your son off the Cape and to Dana-Farber in an hour?"

"You are correct," I replied. There was another long pause.

"Mr. Dezell, we can make that happen," the EMT said in a thick Boston accent.

"Thank you," I said gratefully. "Now, here's the scoop: My wife knows none of this is happening, and her immediate reaction is going to be *'There's no way he can go out to the Cape. What about the traffic on a Sunday afternoon? What happens if he needed to get to the hospital for an emergency in Boston on a Sunday?'*"

The paramedic paused again.

"Mr. Dezell, please let your wife know that if something were to occur and your son did need to get to Boston, no one, and I mean no one, can get him into Boston faster than we can."

"Even on a Sunday?" I asked.

"We'd be like a hot knife through buttah (he meant "butter" but his thick Boston accent blurred that), even on a Sunday."

"You're the best, my man. I will be in touch."

With that hurdle out of the way, I called Dr. Jennifer Levine, Frank's pediatric oncologist at Columbia University Medical Center.

"Oh my God," she said with a laugh. "I can't believe you are still focused on this."

"You'd better believe I am. This trip will mean everything in the world to Frankie. It will be good for his two brothers, too. It will be good for the whole family."

"Okay," Dr. Levine said. "Let me get this set up with Dana-Farber. My only requirement is that you find a nurse who can draw his blood each day."

Feeling on top of the world, I promised: "I will make that happen."

I contacted a visiting nurse service on Cape Cod and explained what we needed. A sweet, retired nurse named Bunny was assigned to stop by each day and draw blood as needed.

The next hurdle was with the clinic. We had to wait for confirmation that Frankie's body wasn't ready for more chemo.

The clinic staff drew his blood and found that because of the sluggishness in his recovery, we had a five-day "pass" before he could endure another chemo treatment. At this point, Jane Dunleavy, the lead nurse practitioner, knew about my rescue plan.

"So, looks like you have about five days home again before you can come back. Do you have anything planned?" she asked with a wink.

"Yes, as matter of fact we do. 02659," I replied.

"Well, you enjoy yourself."

Frankie overheard the conversation. "What's 02659?" he asked.

"I will tell you later."

As we drove away, I looked at him, all bald and wearing his little New England Patriots hat.

"So," I told Frankie, "they indicated we have five days before you get readmitted to the hospital for another chemo treatment."

"I know," he replied.

"So, what are we going to do for five days?"

"I don't know. What's that 659 number you were talking to Jane about?"

"It's 02659, Frank, and that's the ZIP Code for the Cape. If we have five days off, I think we should go out to Chatham. What do you think?"

His eyes twinkled.

"Does Mom know?"

"No, but we'll tell her soon."

We phoned Keri at the house. "How did the appointment go," her voice inquired over the car's speaker.

"As expected, Frankie's counts are too low for them to give him more chemo."

"So, you're coming home?"

"Actually, no," I replied.

"What are you talking about? Why aren't you coming home?"

"Frank and I realized we have five days off. So, rather than sitting out at the house AGAIN for five days, we have decided…"

Frankie's eyes were bright.

"We're going to Cape Cod," our son blurted out.

There was a measured pause.

"What are you talking about? You cannot go to Cape Cod, Frankie!"

"We are on our way now!" Frankie proclaimed. "Who is going to stop us?"

"You cannot go to Cape Cod!"

Frankie was laughing excitedly.

"Try and stop us," he taunted.

"Jim, what is he talking about???" Keri asked sternly.

"Actually, we have been given authorization to go," I replied.

"By whom?"

"Dr. Levine…"

"But you can't…what if something…"

"We have Dana-Farber all set up. She has a doctor there 'on call' just in case Frankie needs to come. They know Frankie's story…"

"What about the traffic…we can't go because if there's traffic getting off the Cape…"

"Already taken care of. I spoke to Chatham's ambulance unit. If we have to get to Boston and to Dana Farber, they'll be happy to take us."

"That won't work on a Sunday afternoon."

"Already discussed that. Chatham EMT said he'd get Frankie to Boston faster than a plane, even on a Sunday."

I could tell there was still a lot of concern. Actually, Keri was livid that she was put on the spot like that.

"Look," I said. "Dr. Levine knows we're headed into a war zone with these next rounds of treatment. She also recognizes this will be great for the whole family, to have some normalcy, even if for five days. So pack the bags, let's go out there, and let's have some fun."

"Dr. Levine said that? I don't know...," Keri stated with hesitation. "This doesn't seem right..."

"Well, you can think about it all you want, but Frank and I are headed there right now. We have the green light from his doctor. Frank and I agree. We don't need two invites to go out to the Cape..."

Frankie was beaming and nodding.

That night, the entire family arrived on Cape Cod.

Normalcy never felt so good. We played football on the beach. We rode go-karts. We went crabbing. We devoured s'mores in the back yard and visited each of our favorite haunts. It was a glorious break after everything our family had been through over three months.

While we braced for the next rounds of chemo treatments for Frankie, we were also quite conscious that Max and James needed to have as much balance to their lives as we could provide.

After our getaway, Frankie and I headed to New York for his next chemo regimen. Keri took James and Max to their grandparents' house near Boston. The grandparents then took the boys to an uncle's summer house on Lake Winnipesaukee in New Hampshire for the final days of the summer.

It was a prescient break before transitioning from an unusual summer. And the next phases of treatment made the first ones seem like a walk through a park.

After the kidnapping to Cape Cod, Frank, Max and James ventured to the shore for some crabbing.

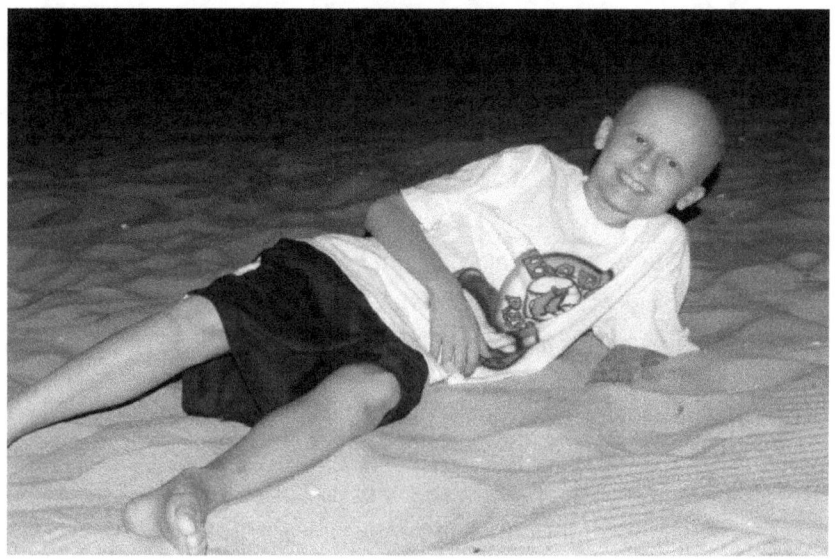

Frankie enjoying some late-night beach time in between treatments.

Fighting cancer: "The Heavy Artillery comes out"

The doctors had warned us. September 2010 was going to be brutal. On top of the other chemo side effects, Frankie would experience the ugliness of infections, mouth sores, muscle pain and lethargy.

Early into the regimen, a work colleague asked how he was doing.

"Do you remember in the movie *The Wizard of Oz*, when the flying monkeys get ahold of the Scarecrow and rip all the stuffing out of him?" I replied.

The colleague nodded.

"Well, Frankie's like the scarecrow right now."

One concoction of chemo and drugs left him arthritic and unable to walk. Another set left his mouth riddled with ulcers and open sores. He could eat only soft foods and soup during this period. He would purposefully eat very slowly to avoid aggravating the sores. During one meal, Max and I watched him slowly and methodically take each bite—it was like witnessing a 100-year-old man have his last meal. Poor Frankie was only 8 years old.

Three years before Frankie's diagnosis, I had started an NFL Youth Football league in our town. James, Max and Frankie all played in it. What had started with 38 kids in 2007 grew to a program with more than 375 youngsters. Within a few years, between a full-time job and Frankie's illness, I found it burdensome to continue managing. But I knew the continuity would be good for each of our kids, so I remained with the program.

When he wasn't getting treatments, Frankie was thrilled to still participate in the league. He showed up to the practices and games bald and gray but loving every minute of playing football. He wasn't allowed to attend school during his chemo regimen—he had a tutor—so the comradery of being a teammate was a dose of joy.

This round of chemo, however, had ignited an internal fungus. Every afternoon, Keri would attach through the IV port in his chest a "medicine ball" filled with an antifungal drug. Regardless, Frankie would still show up to football practice every Friday with the medicine ball shoved deep into his pocket. As he ran down the field, the IV lines flopped in the wind. He didn't care. He was thrilled to feel normal and just do what the other kids did.

As autumn progressed, Frankie adapted to the harsher treatments-and was doing incredibly well recovering from each round. Life was almost idyllic. Nonetheless, the grotesqueness and ugliness of the disease lurched forward. But the cancer didn't know an army of angels was lining up to defeat it, led by my wife, the Head Saint. Keri wrote in her blog in early November:

A beautiful Frankie story, but, a heavy week...
November 3, 2010, 11:49 a.m.

Ironically, last week was supposed to be an "easier" week and just as it should be, from our beautiful Frankie's perspective, it was.

As many of you know, during this phase some of Frankie's chemotherapy is administered via the outpatient clinic at the hospital. However, there are some mornings and evenings that our beloved visiting nurse, Mary Ellen, comes to our home to administer chemotherapy. :) The ability to receive treatment via the outpatient clinic and at home has done wonders for Frankie's mind, body and soul. It has allowed Frankie to get the chemo that he needs while reaping the psychological benefits of being home.

Throughout last week's treatment, Frankie remained determined and focused on attending Friday's football practice and Saturday's game. However, we knew by Friday's practice that he would have received 5 days of chemo (a.m. and p.m.) to be concluded on Friday at 8 p.m. Taking this into consideration, it just didn't seem possible that he'd be able to attend. But knowing that we can never go by Frankie's determination and SPIRIT alone, we reached out to Dr. Levine... "Keri, let's see how he's feeling on Friday, but you know, this is the BIONIC BOY we're talking about! If he's feeling up to it and he wants to play, there's no harm. Just watch to be sure he doesn't overdo it."

Come Friday night (after instructing himself to take two breaks), his knit Patriots hat pulled over his little, bald head and a week's worth of chemo running through his veins, Frankie took to the field ready, willing and able to kick some @$$! Just like he said he would! That's our warrior! Sorry, but sometimes the only words that will do are expletives! And right now, is one of those times. It is during times like these he takes our breath away. GO Frankie GO!!!

And THANK YOU for keeping our baby close to your heart and in your prayers. PLEASE KEEP IT UP! Frankie is "living proof of your prayers" and GOD is listening...

I don't typically share the negatives of this disease. It is our belief that in doing so, you're helping to ignite ~~cancer~~'s flame, giving it exactly what it needs and craves to take hold and grow further. Simultaneously, we also recognize that one has to fully acknowledge "it" in all of its "gory" to snuff it out completely.

So, here we are. At this moment within our journey, it is

imperative that we do just that. Since May, we've spent many hours/days/weeks in the clinic, so the environment is not new to us. During last week's visits, I stepped away from our own journey and realistically took in what was happening around me: Dedicated nurses were comforting and caring for several pediatric patients with moderate to extreme needs; babies and children cried as nurses administered chemotherapies and powerful medicines to save their lives; moms and dads wore worried, tired, and distraught expressions while waiting for lab results for hours on end.

And then there was Jewel, whose name I didn't know until last week. During prior clinic visits, she and I had exchanged pleasantries, but that was about it. I always thought of Jewel as an attractive woman, with a radiant smile. So when I saw her looking uncharacteristically disheveled, it was noticeable. Her 13-year-old old son, Kelvin, in treatment for a year, had recently relapsed. They had tried a variety of treatments and she was told there was nothing more they could do. She said it so quietly and without expression that my eyes immediately filled with tears. I know that we didn't know each other well, but how do you hear words like that and not reach out? I hugged her so tightly and when I did, Jewel hugged me back just as tight. I thought, I will not release this hug first... this was her hug to hold on to for as long as she needed. I then kissed her cheek, as if through my kiss I could will her son to be rid of this ugly, ugly ~~cancer~~. Enough, I thought. Enough. Then I did the only thing I know to do and I graciously implore the same from each of you... "What are your names? I will pray for you and for your son."

May we pray that this disease and all its ugliness be eradicated

so the Kelvin's, the Grace's, the Melony's, the Frankie's and countless others, are freed from the reins of ~~cancer~~.
** Please email me your thoughts and/or prayers for Kelvin & his mom, Jewel. I'll print your words and give them to Jewel to use as a reminder that we are here to catch them should they fall. Just as our beautiful friend Marisa did for us. XO

OUR LITTLE WARRIOR WILL WIN NO QUESTION ABOUT IT!
With a heavy heart and much love,
Keri, Jim, James, Max and Frankie

The responses for Kelvin and for Jewel were incredible:

Lolly Quagliarello
November 3, 2010, 12:19 p.m.
Dear Keri... I just finished wiping my eyes... this entry really pulled at my heartstrings... Jack commented that isn't a warrior a soldier, I said yes it can mean that, but it also refers to a fighter, hero, battler and a champion... Frankie, Jewel and Kelvin and their families all embody the above attributes. We love you all and are ALWAYS in our prayers. God Bless all those battling cancer. xo
The Q's

Ellen O'Brien
November 3, 2010, 2:30 p.m.
Keri, you are an angel. I know in my heart that God put you near Jewel in that moment because you have a natural, comforting way about you. Thank you for all you do, and for who you are. We love you and admire you so much! I will keep Jewel and all the others in my prayers. God bless you, and your beautiful

family, especially our main man, the fighting machine, FRANKIE!!!! Love, Ellen & John xoxoxoxox

Sally Green
November 3, 2010, 2:54 p.m.
Keri, it's so hard to write the correct words for all of the emotions this stuff brings out. Joy and hope for you guys, tears and empathy for Jewel, there really ARE no words for this stuff, and clearly you know that. A hug and prayers are the little comfort someone might be able to give, and of course can't ease the pain the way you want them to. Thank you for being there for her and of COURSE Kelvin and family are included in our prayers from now on. These messages are always great reminders of what is important in life. Thank you so so so much for doing them and filling us in and bringing comfort to Jewel and just being YOU. Love you all, Sal

This is only a sample of the replies. Keri received hundreds of other prayers and responses for Jewel and Kelvin. She printed them all, put them in an album (titled Kelvin's Angels) and delivered it to Jewel and Kelvin, who were extremely grateful and touched. She and Keri continued to see each other several times a week at the clinic and they remain friends today.

As youth football season ended, the basketball season began. Frank signed up for the Catholic youth basketball program at our church. Of course, he was the only bald kid running up and down the courts and garnered much support that season. During one game, he took a floater shot from the outside and it went in— nothing but net. The crowd erupted like it was the winning shot of the NBA Finals.

Frankie had no idea about the fervor and support behind him. His determination, energy and drive were infectious and inspiring to many. A day nurse helped him when he was home, and she fell in love with his courage and verve. We had employed a tutor to use as much as Frankie could tolerate, to help him with his schoolwork. She was also captivated by his charisma.

One day around Christmastime, Frankie was at the hospital on an outpatient basis getting chemo and a group of firefighters from a firehouse in Harlem came in with gifts for the children. They spotted Frankie wearing his New England Patriots hat and wardrobe, and began telling him that he was confused, in the wrong state and should be wearing New York Jets or New York Giants attire.

Frankie proceeded to "chirp" and "trash talk" those two New York teams, and a friendship was ignited with all the first responders that remains to this day.

Firefighters are unique and remarkable people (think about it— how many people do you know who run *into* burning buildings to save others). In their limited spare time, a group of firefighters from Engine 84/Ladder 34 (in the Washington Heights section of Manhattan) and their wives created a charitable group called the Lil' Bravest Foundation. This exceptional charity provides a safe, happy space and monetary aid, for ill children and their families around the country.

All the outpouring of love, compassion and concern was remarkable. At the same time, we also witnessed the glaring ignorance of a few. In February 2011, I had a business lunch and one of my colleagues who attended mentioned Frankie's situation. The businessman who joined us then spent the next 45 minutes talking about how devastated he would be if his child was ever diagnosed with cancer! I had to tolerate this guy talking about himself for nearly an hour. By the end of lunch, I was more and more annoyed and distant from the conversation. Finally, he looked over at me and, almost sobbing, started a flurry of questions:

"So, were you thoroughly depressed when they told you he had cancer?"

"Were you terrified?"

"I would have been terrified. I would be no use to anyone. I would be crying for days. Did you cry?"

To each question, with my irritation rising, I tersely responded no.

"You must be so strong. I watch you sitting here and can't imagine how strong you are..."

This comment further annoyed me.

"Strength has nothing to do with it," I cut in. "This is not about 'me'—it is about our son. My boy was diagnosed with cancer. Fear, sadness and depression are negative emotions. Why am I going to let these enter the orbit when all we want is to get him well, and all we want is to destroy cancer?"

I hastily ordered the check and left.

As much as we tried to normalize things, it was usually beyond our control; the savagery of cancer kept showing up. I heard about many of Frankie's friends going on their play dates, heading to that next birthday party, getting ready for their basketball games and signing up for baseball, and it hurt.

At the cancer clinic, it was a much different story.

In early spring 2011, close to the one-year anniversary of Frankie's leukemia diagnosis, Keri wrote an update in her journal:

Kelvin Thomas

My heart is heavy and my words are few, but so many of you have asked for an update on Kelvin. He was released from the hospital on Thursday and has been home with his family. He remains under both hospice care and the care of his ever-prayerful mom, Jewel.
In December, one of Kelvin's dreams came true.... He not only attended but, through a wonderful charity, the Tom Coughlin Jay Fund, Kelvin flew with the NY Giants football team for the game against the Minnesota Vikings...AND Yes, it was THAT GAME. The game where the Viking's Stadium roof caved in forcing the team and Kelvin :) to leave Minnesota for the Detroit Lion's stadium. Well, after many gasps (thinking Kelvin's dream was shattered) I shed happy tears. As it turns out, this worked to Kelvin's advantage. Kelvin had 48 hours of travel time and dinners with his beloved team—the NY GIANTS! No accident there! All meant to be! That was for Kelvin! Then last week, Tom Coughlin (the NY Giants coach) heard about Kelvin's decline and paid him a personal hospital

visit. He gifted Kelvin a signed NY Giants' helmet and jersey stitched with Kelvin's last name—Thomas #1.

Enjoy this clip filming Kelvin getting the game ball...and thank you GOD for giving Kelvin and his MOM this magical moment. http://www.nfl.com/videos/new-york-giants/09000d5d81ce7336/Coughlin-gives-game-ball-hope

In the five minutes from when I began typing this entry to now...Jewel phoned. Kelvin has just passed. I'm so deeply sorry for having to share such news. Please keep the Thomas family in your prayers. I can't even begin to imagine their pain. I am at a loss for words.

With love, thanks and in prayer,
Keri

Keri and Frankie witnessed firsthand 13-year-old Kelvin's tragic decline to cancer. As I talked with Frankie about the loss, I felt so sad for Kelvin, his family and for Frankie to have experienced this.

It was a cruel time. Winter was ending, basketball season was wrapping up, and Frankie was missing school and his pals. With my business travel curtailed while Frankie was in treatment, I decided it was time to transform a large, unfinished room over our garage into a recreation room. I took my time, and the other two sons helped me.

This all changed when I got home from work one day.

Frankie greeted me with a smile.

"How was your trip to the clinic today?" I asked him.

"It was good," he answered, still smiling. "Mom and I were talking on the way home, and we started planning my birthday party."

I was a bit perplexed and looked at Keri, who was smirking. His birthday is on April 3, which was five weeks away. "So, you're having a birthday party, Frank?"

"Yes. In between my treatments, the only day that we can do it is on this day because my counts should be okay then."

I kept looking at Frankie, and then at Keri.

"Okay, what do you plan on doing for your birthday, Frankie?"

"I want to take my friends to a Japanese Hibachi restaurant," he replied. "Then, I want to have a sleepover with them."

"Okay. This all sounds good. How many children will be sleeping over?" I inquired.

Frankie started to laugh.

"Twenty-two," he replied.

I was stunned and looked at Keri for feedback. She gave nothing away. "Well, that's not going to work, Frankie. There's nowhere for 22 kids to sleep in the house."

Frankie pointed to the room that I had started remodeling above the garage. "We can if you get that room finished. You need to finish that room," he implored.

Sometimes, parents have to say "no" to children for their own good. And we must be firm. This changes a great deal when the child asking you for something has cancer, is bald and is pleading for your approval. My mind went into high gear: *How in the hell can I get a room that is only 5 percent finished as of right now done in five weeks, while I have a full-time job?* I started thinking out how long it would take me to complete each phase of the room, calculating that if I worked five hours each weeknight and 17 hours on Saturdays and Sundays, I might be able to pull it off.

"Okay, Frankie. I'll get it done. I don't know how, but we'll get it done."

He rejoiced. Keri looked at me like I was out of my mind. Which is arguable.

For the next five weeks, I'd arrive home from a 1.5-hour commute, often at 7:30 p.m., change from my suit to work clothes, and tackle the garage loft to build Frankie his prized room. I would work until 1 a.m. and then get on the computer to figure out what furniture, carpeting, paint colors, televisions, etc. that we needed. On weekends, I often worked 17 hours a day. James and Max helped me as laborers when they could, in between homework and other duties. We'd staple insulation, run ceiling joists, frame new walls and hang sheetrock.

While I am rather handy, I was a horrible foreman to the boys. I appreciated their help, but time was so critical that I never took into consideration their actual ages and that teaching them how to install insulation or pull wires was going to be that much more time-consuming. I was a complete jerk throughout the construction process.

Somehow, we got it all done. We literally had the carpet installed the day before the party and furniture arrived that night. The TV was connected on the day of the sleepover.

And, yes, we took Frankie and 22 of his friends to a Japanese restaurant before they all spent the night in Frankie's treasured loft.

Frankie beamed. All was good.

Jewel and her precious son, Kelvin.

December 2010: New York Giants Coach Tom Coughlin with his buddy Kelvin.

Frank takes control of the offense on the football field. He'd show up with his portable IVs intact.

I guarantee that kid never saw a defender like this one before.

Construction begins on the room for Frankie's birthday bash.

Twenty-two kids (not all pictured) slept over in the recently finished bonus room to celebrate Frank's 9th birthday.

With his firefighter buddies from FDNY Engine 84/Ladder 34, founders of the Lil' Bravest Foundation.

One-Year Mark: "The Crappy Anniversary"

For the one-year anniversary of his diagnosis, Keri had asked Frankie what he wanted to do. It was simple: Have a party and invite guests whom Frankie (not us) would handpick himself.

Keri felt strongly about how our family should mark the one-year anniversary. She thought it was important that we let cancer know we're still here—and we're living, laughing, loving loud and proud—and not running or hiding from cancer.

On May 20, 2011, Frankie's personally chosen guests were invited to attend a dinner while gathered around our backyard fire pit. Keri had requested that each attendee write an open, honest letter to cancer—anything they wanted to convey. It was up to each individual whether to read the letter out loud. Some did, some didn't—but after each reading or acknowledgment, each person threw his or her letter into the fire with the idea that every letter burned would help to extinguish the cancer. Through laughter and some tears, we showed cancer it had no room to breathe here.

Frankie listened intently as the words filled the night air, the flames reflecting in his eyes. It was a powerful, beautiful, therapeutic and healing experience. Cancer didn't exist in those moments, only love.

Keri later posted the original copy of her letter on her blog:

Dear ~~Cancer~~,
One year ago today, we answered an unexpected knock on our door… with arrogance and callousness, you pushed us aside and grabbed hold of our son. Within seconds, life as we knew it was over. You had OUR BABY. We were caught off guard and were made to feel helpless and vulnerable. For those first few hours, we remained captive to your demands. We found ourselves robotically following your lead. We listened intently as YOU dictated your specific instructions. Afraid we might miss something that could jeopardize the life of our son, we always kept you within eyesight. We responded just as you'd planned, better yet, just as you'd expected. We were unknowingly following your plan to the "T." This made you feel indestructible. You were now the force to be reckoned with. You began taunting us, by slowly and methodically tightening your grip on our precious baby, our son. Feeling a sense of helplessness, we began to cry. We began to crumble. We acknowledged your power—and in doing so and without our knowing it, we were relinquishing OUR power to you. This

excited you. Almost immediately, we saw the twinkle in your eyes. Seeing this, we realized we HAD to make a move. NOW. We had to find a way to stop feeding your frenzy. We had to find a way to take back all control. For we knew if we didn't, our baby would be yours forever... and under NO CIRCUMSTANCES would we EVER allow that to happen. EVER.

So, we did the only thing we knew how to do. We did what comes naturally to us and we didn't worry about the consequences. We pulled ourselves up off the floor and we STOOD TALL, being sure to stare YOU back in the eye. OUR EYES NOW GLEAMING, we called to our Lord, our GOD and asked him to join us in our fight. We knew that with GOD by our side, alive and well in our hearts, WE were NOW the force to be reckoned with. YOU DIDN'T STAND A CHANCE. In awe, we watched our then 8-year-old son pick himself back up, stand tall and call on our Lord, our GOD, to join HIM in his fight. Shortly thereafter, you reluctantly began to release your grip and retreat. The power that you had held, if only momentarily, had shifted back into the hands to which it ultimately belonged, to our Lord, our GOD. Knowing this, with fervor and without hesitation, Frankie began to dictate TO YOU the NEW TERMS and CONDITIONS under which you would NOW operate. Frankie did not mince his words. He was strong and he was clear. With the GLEAM NOW shining brightly in his EYES, he wasted no time being sure to tell you who NOW HELD THE POWER. Clearly and distinctly, you could hear Frankie's voice, "You picked the wrong body to mess with, ~~cancer~~! I see you. Now, YOU'RE screaming—LET ME OUT! Now it is YOU who is scared. It is YOU who wants out of me!"

~~Cancer~~, let me be clear... you do not hold the power...God does. You do not have the control...Frankie does. We will not bow to you. You will cower to us. We will fight with fierce determination...we will love, harder than we ever have. We will laugh, loud and strong. You do not have GOD on your side, alive and well within your heart and YOU NEVER WILL. Your intent is evil. Your intent is to harm. Your intent is to instill fear. Your intent is to remove GOD from the equation. Well, guess what??? That HAS NOT and WILL NOT EVER HAPPEN. You will forever be alone... which means, YOU DON'T STAND A CHANCE. YOU NEVER DID. GO FRANKIE GO!!!!!
THANK YOU GOD. ALWAYS AND FOREVER.
KERI, JIM, JAMES, MAX AND FRANKIE

Kenneth Shea
May 21, 2011, 9:50 a.m.
All I can say is, Inspirational, simply Inspirational...the Dezell Family rocks, and no foe of the Dezells will ever stand a chance. Frankie, you are the best. Love, the Sheas

Sharon Moffett
May 21, 2011, 7:06 p.m.
What a beautiful letter this is. God truly listens to those who pray. Our faith has to be strong, to butt this horrible disease in the head and destroy it. No doubt about it, you surely will win this battle. Keep up the great work! Go Frankie Go....you can and will win this battle against the evil one.
Our Lord is standing by your side. He is surely listening to all of the prayers being said for you. God Bless You All. With Love And Our Prayers—Sharon

Connie Herrell
May 21, 2011, 12:15 p.m.
Keri, my heart is moved again and again by what you write and share with us through CaringBridge. We love you all, there is no denying God's presence and the Holy Spirit that exists within your family. Connie

Mary Ellen Lavelle
May 21, 2011, 11:54 a.m.
Keri, Thanks for the gift you have given us each time you write a new Frankie update. You are amazing, your thoughts and words are inspirational. The Frankie Message Collection is waiting to be collated and published! It will be so helpful to the families of children newly diagnosed with cancer. It will help them stay focused on what is happening in their lives and how to get through it. You and the Dezells have been there and done that! I share your belief in the amazing power of prayer and your joy in seeing Frankie return to being a happy, healthy 9-year-old! ME

Arjan van de Wall
May 21, 2011, 1:43 p.m.
Dezells you are amazing, and Keri you are a very inspirational writer and role model for any mom/family who has to go through an ordeal like this. Keep on going strong and keep up the fight. You are all in our hearts and prayers. Special xoxoxox for Frankie!!! Fleur, Arjan and kids

5/20/11 marked Frankie's one-year anniversary of his diagnosis. His personally chosen guests each wrote a letter to cancer, read it out loud, and then threw it in a fire pit with the idea that each one burned would help to extinguish the cancer.

Year 2: "Scintillating through the Slog"

The spring and summer of 2012 progressed steadily, and we did everything we could between the treatments to enjoy ourselves and love our three boys. Frankie still faced nasty side effects from the chemo, steroids and ongoing spinal taps. Nonetheless, Mr. Frankie persevered and even returned to school sporadically as his drug regimens and wellness allowed. He was ecstatic to have a semblance of normalcy and hang out with his friends. He continued to play football, even when he was in pain from steroids and spinal taps. His courage and fortitude were amazing and inspirational to witness.

My employer had been somewhat accommodating since Frank's

ordeal began, and at times I would take a day off to help Keri and take Frank to the clinic where, week after week, he would have the chemo drugs delivered into his fragile veins.

During one visit, I counted eight other children getting their chemo regimen. All were younger than 15. Some were babies or toddlers.

I kept glancing at everyone. They were emotionless and stared off into a gloomy space. You knew they wished they could be anywhere but there. Each child in the clinic that day was going through the savagery of cancer, and you could see in their faces the weathered pain of immense disappointment, of consistently getting stuck with a shitty hand at the poker table. It is a difficult diagnosis, especially for a child. And the protracted treatments and medicines used to control it, many times for years, are toxic.

It broke my heart to see people so young have to encounter that reality.

And, amidst all the messiness in our lives, Frankie turned 10. We continued to fight on, looking forward to the treatments ending that summer, and the decrease in Frankie's hospital appointments.

In the spring, the Make-A-Wish organization, which orchestrates and fulfills the wishes of children with critical illnesses, interviewed Frank. In my humble opinion, it is one of the most remarkable charitable organizations in the world because its entire focus is bringing joy and gratification to sick children.

When Make-A-Wish organizers interviewed Frank, they did it one-on-one so that no parents or siblings could influence him.

Another family had nominated him for a "wish." The representatives came to our house to ask him what kind of a wish he wanted. Later, Frankie burst into my bedroom where I was reading a magazine.

"So, Make-A-Wish says they can send me to a special area at Disney World. Maybe I should go to Disney?"

I thought for a moment.

"Frankie, you have already been to Disney World, and we're blessed in a lot of ways that we can probably go there again. Why don't you do something different than something you have already done?"

He nodded and ran off.

About 15 minutes later, he returned.

"Remember when we were in the hospital and saw that safari expedition on the Discovery Channel? I want to go to South Africa on a safari."

"Okay, Frank, that's fine, but do you know that if we left now to fly to South Africa, we're on a plane until tomorrow at 4 p.m.? The plane trip is 18 hours."

He didn't like hearing that and returned to his interview.

A short time later, he was at my door again.

"I decided what I am going to do..."

"Great. What, Frank?"

"I am going to meet Tom Brady," referring to the New England Patriots quarterback.

"Well, Frankie, I think that is great. Is that something that is difficult to set up?"

Apparently, for Make-A-Wish, it wasn't. The wheels went into motion and Make-A-Wish launched its effort to make his dream come true.

Before Frankie finished the last of his chemo regimens a few weeks later, doctors wanted to wallop him with drugs several more times. There was a window of time in early summer when Keri took the other two boys to Cape Cod, but Frankie needed to stay in New York for treatments. We felt badly that Frank couldn't join them, so I decided to take time off work for us to have an exclusive four-day weekend. We had a blast. We went fishing for frogs. We spent a day at a water park riding crazy slides. We went to the movies. We went into Manhattan, ate pizza, and spent the night. We knew Keri, Max and James would make s'mores over a fire pit at the Cape Cod house, so we found a restaurant in New York City that served s'mores and had our own version on Broadway.

A few weeks later, in late July, doctors concluded that Frankie was in remission, ended his chemo treatments and removed the IV port from his chest. Keri posted the news that morning.

FRANKIE's TEAM-- You're not done yet... :)
July 23, 2012

It is 5:25 a.m. and today marks 2 years, 2 months, 2 days, 19 hours, 25 minutes and 6 seconds since Frankie began what will

hopefully be the hardest and longest battle of his life, for his life. It is our hope that today will also mark a new beginning to our new "normal."

At 10:20 a.m. TODAY, a surgeon is scheduled to remove the port from Frankie's chest. The port, although effective, is no longer required. It no longer serves a purpose, as its sole purpose was to receive & deliver chemo, and guess what???? THAT IS NO LONGER NECESSARY! Frankie is pumped and is ready to move on! Go Frankie Go!

Once the surgeon has successfully removed the port, Dr. Levine will step in to perform what should be Frankie's LAST Bone Marrow Aspiration. The Bone Marrow Aspiration (formal results come back in a couple of days to a week) is necessary to REAFFIRM that our Frankie REMAINS ~~CANCER~~ FREE. NO DOUBT baby NO DOUBT!!!

We have been so incredibly blessed to have each of you to call on throughout this journey and from the bottom of our hearts we thank you, but we're not done yet... please continue to send our baby your most positive intentions—this morning especially. Please keep him close to your heart and in your prayers for safekeeping. We treasure your choosing to be part of our journey.

Thank you, GOD, for your continued guidance and love.
With gratitude and with love,
Keri, Jim, James, Max and Frank

This was truly a major event. His grandparents, Keri's sister, Erin, and her son Joseph arrived from Boston. We all went to the hospital for the procedure, during which Frank was knocked out by anesthesia.

Hundreds of messages erupted in cheers to the most recent news from Keri's blog. A sample:

Terry Gauld
July 23, 2012, 12:37 p.m.
To all the Dezells, AMEN! Not a dry eye will read your entry, Keri. You have all endured so much for too long, and Frankie is everyone's hero! Church is a definite today to thank God and ask for his continued guidance. His love is always there, as is ours. xo Rich and Terry

Valerie Stasiak
July 23, 2012, 12:54 p.m.
Good Morning Keri - and I do mean GOOD MORNING!! This is the day we've all waited and prayed for - the glorious day when Frankie can go back to being a "kid" - enjoying all the "normal" stuff that comes along with growing up. The profound difference is that Frankie now knows the challenge of navigating through a horrific disease. He thankfully knows the healing process inside and out! He knows in his heart the true meaning of life - it's the love that matters. It's God that matters. During all those dark, frightening times, Frankie saw through YOU what is possible with faith, hope and love. You showed us all that there is no "fear" that is greater than faith. It's been a privilege to be a tiny part of this miraculous journey you shared with us. I will continue to send love, light, prayers and hugs to you, Frankie and your whole family. You did it, Keri!! You stayed the course

and got everyone through!! Frankie is my hero and YOU are my hero. I am quite sure you were what God had in mind when he created "mothers." Love to you always, Keri!! And hugs all around for all the Dezells!!!

Alessandra Hernandez
July 23, 2012, 1:54 p.m.
I am so, so happy this nightmare is finally over! You all must be ecstatic!!! Frankie, you have always been so amazingly strong even though you've been battling an incredibly powerful adversary. You have shown how tenacious you can be, determined to never give up. And always with the most beautiful smile. There are so many people that proudly look up to you. You are a true superhero. Mom, Dad, James & Max, you have been an unwavering source of power. Your faith, your beliefs, your prayers, your support have been constant and have made, I'm sure, many who doubted believe again. You are one of, if not the nicest, loving family we know. We are honored to have had the chance to know you over the past many years. We rejoice in your victory! All our love, Alessandra, Russell, Daniel, Gabe & Serena

A few weeks later, we held an outdoor surprise party for Frankie with family and friends called "FRANKIE's DEPORTED PARTY." Some clever friends made T-shirts sporting his face and a cancel stamp. But Frankie's biggest thrill was still to come. I mentioned earlier that Make-A-Wish had interviewed Frank in the spring. In November, the organization fulfilled its promise, and Keri shared the announcement online:

"A MEETING OF THE CHAMPIONS"
December 5, 2012, 3:42 a.m.

At long last, our little Warrior was able to partake in his MAKE-A-WISH event. On 11-16-12, a "tricked" out stretch limo arrived to pick up our little warrior and his "tag-alongs"—US! Headed to The Gillette Stadium in Foxboro, Massachusetts, we sat back to enjoy our ride in style! With music blaring, lights flashing and celebratory glasses clinking, we were off!!!

Our magical journey included a 3-night, 4-day stay at the infamous PATRIOTS PLACE; a tour of the Stadium, the field and the locker rooms; AND tickets to watch the Pats vs. Indianapolis game! And those were just the "extras"... Frankie's real wish came true when he got to meet his IDOL—TOM BRADY. Actually, "meet" is an understatement. Frankie, playing QB, had Tom go out for a long pass. Imagine that??!! Then Frankie "almost" beat Tom in a 40-yard dash, after having chatted him up to find out about the latest games, trying to get the inside "skinny" on any upcoming games! Frankie had the time of his life—as did we all. THEN, as if that weren't enough, the MAKE-A-WISH FOUNDATION AND THE PATRIOTS had another surprise for Frankie and gang...the entire team came over to introduce themselves to our champion! That was over the top! OVER-THE-TOP!!! Oh, and let's not forget, New England Patriot's Coach Bill Belichick pulled Frankie in for a big hug to tell him that HE is HIS hero for whooping ~~cancer~~'s butt!

Back at home, reminiscing about our magical weekend, Jim asked Frankie, "Frankie on a scale of 1 to 10 [with 10 being the best], what would you rate the MAKE-A-WISH WEEKEND?" A slight pause before Frankie looks up and says, "A million." How do you put words to that?

With many deep and heartfelt thank you's to the MAKE-A-WISH FOUNDATION...The PATRIOTS...and TOM BRADY for creating such a magical weekend for Frankie and the other 3 Make-A-Wish families. Beautiful. It was a meeting of champions for sure!!!

Please keep our Warrior in your prayers!!! They are ALWAYS WELCOME and NEEDED.   Love-- Jim, Keri, James, Max and Frankie

Frankie hanging out with Tom Brady and Rob Gronkowski

Bill Belichick showing his respect for Frankie (both moments courtesy of Make-A-Wish).

The Make-A-Wish event was a well-deserved reward after everything Frankie had been through. This charity is one of the most remarkable and special organizations in the world, and its efforts and work on behalf of critically sick children are as important as the medicine children are given to be well.

Frankie's treatments, side effects and hospital stays had lasted for two and a half years. After his dream of meeting Tom Brady became reality, the months and seasons flowed. Frankie returned to school. He continued to play sports and got tested often at the hospital to monitor possible residual side effects from the treatments and check for risk of a relapse.

Cancer had made us closer as a family. It opened our world to take advantage of every opportunity. We took more excursions. We traveled to Italy and to France. We frequented Cape Cod.

As much as we celebrated and tried to put cancer behind us, however, there was still an understated, nagging shadow lurking.

We had overcome cancer—that couldn't be forgotten. Yet, we had been abruptly and violently awakened by it.

No matter how much fun and spontaneity we embraced while Frankie was in remission, we were forever cognizant and haunted that cancer could return at any point, and with a violent ferocity.

The Rematch: "Numbing Period, Part II"

On Friday, June 13, 2014, Keri had been monitoring Frankie for a couple of months because he was complaining of the same stomach issues he had experienced before his cancer diagnosis. She had taken him to the pediatrician and was in touch with his oncologist off and on about the various symptoms. Nothing was glaring, but still the signs kept gnawing at her.

Though Keri was concerned, I just wouldn't immerse myself into a land of worry and false alarms. That morning, after speaking with Dr. Levine, Keri followed her suggestion to have Frank's blood drawn at the local doctor's office.

I had been on a long business trip to western Pennsylvania and returned home about 6 p.m. that Friday the 13th. Frankie and his brothers were outside playing. I walked around the house trying to find Keri. She was upstairs in our bedroom on the phone with Frankie's oncologist, whispering. She was pale and nodded her head repeatedly to me as I walked in. I stood there confused. She pulled the phone away, covered the mouthpiece, looked into my eyes and whispered tearily:

"It's back."

I was filled with rage and it consumed me more than my fury after Frankie's first diagnosis in 2010. Now, at age 53, I had been through my share of trauma. My father abused me when I was a child. I had drug and alcohol problems as a teenager. I was on a plane that flew into New York City the morning of September 11, 2001. From my perspective, I had crossed paths with evil before: None of that compared to hearing my child's cancer had returned.

"What?" I asked.

Keri nodded. "It's back."

I frantically paced the floor. "May I please speak with Dr. Levine?"

Keri handed me the phone. "Couldn't these test results be inaccurate and wrong?" I repeatedly asked the doctor.

"We can double-check at Columbia tomorrow," Dr. Levine told me.

My denial continued. "He was scoring goals last week at a lacrosse game. He's out playing on a trampoline right now. He looks great."

Dr. Levine indicated there was a slim possibility the lab results could be wrong. She said the best thing was to bring Frankie to Columbia the next day and run the tests. I agreed.

Keri and I stumbled around the house not sure what we were going to do over the next 60 minutes, let alone the next coming months. We began to acknowledge that cancer was going to savagely invade our world again. We learned that our only option for eradicating the enemy was for Frankie to endure a bone marrow transplant, which has complexities on its own.

The revelation sucked the life out of us.

Given everything we had just heard, we decided not to say anything to Frankie or his brothers. Instead, we proceeded with our "normal" Friday night ritual of pizza and a movie. However, we did turn it up a notch to let ourselves laugh and love a little harder—not sure when we would be able to enjoy our next Friday night pizza routine.

So, I ordered the food and Frankie chose a completely inappropriate, raunchy R-rated comedy. Knowing the likely road ahead of us, we gave in to his request rather easily. We just wanted to see him happy and laughing.

The rest of the evening Keri and I were numb. The movie helped to distract us and afterward we talked with the boys about how inappropriately funny it was. I said a prayer when I went to bed that the lab had made a mistake.

The next day, we explained to Frankie that Columbia needed to run more tests because he hadn't been feeling well. Dr. Levine met us in a small triage area at the pediatric emergency room and engaged in banter with Frankie. I could tell she was concerned and cautious. She left after a few minutes, and we kept Frankie occupied with some silly stories and jokes.

About a half-hour later, I saw Dr. Levine outside the room with Keri looking over the lab results. Both were distraught. It was now confirmed: The cancer was back and it was attacking him with a vengeance. Once again, my entire body surged with rage. I felt like a caged animal, pacing like a wolf in a zoo.

Keri and Dr. Levine discussed how they would tell Frankie and went into the triage room. They explained he'd had a relapse and that once again the cancer was coming at him aggressively.

Frankie sobbed uncontrollably and his body was visibly shaking. He looked at Dr. Levine and cried out:

"Am I going to die?"

Our beautiful, amazing, perfect child asked—for the second time in his short life—something that no parent ever wants to hear. Keri responded immediately to the panic taking over. She knelt in front of him and put her hands on his shaking knees. Looking forcefully into his eyes, she said, "NO, FRANKIE! NO! YOU'RE NOT GOING TO DIE!"

Sensing this would be the optimal time for her to intercede, Dr. Levine rolled her chair over to Frankie and placed her hands on his trembling body. "Frankie, remember when you had cancer the last time? I had a lot of tricks in my bag to use on cancer. Well, guess what? I only used this many tricks [she made a tiny gesture with her fingers to illustrate], which means I have a whole BIG BAG of tricks left to use." This time she spread her arms wide.

Frankie continued to sob. I stayed quiet and pictured how many hospital walls I could break down with all my rage. And I kept thinking: *How is this happening AGAIN? Why is this happening again?*

Dr. Levine and Keri hugged Frankie as he cried. It was heartbreaking.

After Keri and the doctor left the triage to start the process for Frankie's readmission, he and I were alone. We didn't speak for about five minutes. I paced frantically and envisioned knocking down a wall with one violent punch. Frankie cried softly.

I searched for what to say. We finally made eye contact, and sadness and fear stared back at me. As with the diagnosis of cancer more than four years ago, I did not want him to be afraid. I knelt on one knee and held his hands.

"I know this is upsetting, Frank."

He cried louder.

"And I know this sucks.

"Four years ago, Frankie, you valiantly and heroically fought cancer. You took it into the ring, went 15 rounds with it, followed all the rules, and you knocked it down. You knocked it out."

His tears dropped on my arm and leg as I knelt before him.

"But, now, Frankie, it's back. Shitty, nasty cancer has snuck back into our lives. And, as you heard Dr. Levine say, it's coming at you...and it is **coming at you hard**."

I squeezed his hands.

"So, it's no longer in the ring, Frank. It's picking a fight with you outside of it. You fought it like a gentleman before, but cancer snuck up from behind and sucker punched you. So, it's now turned this into a street fight."

I locked eyes with him.

"And you want to know what is cool about a street fight, Frank? There are no fucking rules. There are NO fucking rules."

I began sobbing with him as rage filled my body.

"We are going to hit this with everything we have, Frankie.

We're going to punch it. We're going to gouge it. We'll throw rocks. We're going to break bottles on it. This is guerilla warfare, Frank. We are in the mud. We are in the jungles. And there are *NO RULES,* and we will do everything to massacre this, and we will destroy this."

I hugged and kissed him. Dr. Levine and Keri returned, and the attention shifted to getting him admitted to the pediatric cancer ward of the hospital. We knew he would be there initially for a month, probably longer. We also knew he'd be there most of the summer as they prepared him for a bone marrow transplant.

The rest of the day was hectic and eerily familiar. We filled out reams of paperwork and saw so many of the same nurses whom we thought—and had hoped—we'd never see again. They began giving Frankie loads of steroids to combat the cancer's aggressiveness. It was a weekend, so the hospital staff was limited. Before we knew it, it was approaching midnight.

During Frankie's first bout with cancer, doctors had installed an IV port on the right side of his chest to administer medicines. A port is a small device about the size of a half-dollar coin. It's used to draw blood and dispense treatments, including intravenous fluids, blood transfusions, nutritional supplements, or drugs such as chemotherapy and antibiotics. The main advantage of this vein-access device was that medications were delivered directly into the port, eliminating the need for numerous daily needle pricks.

This time, however, his medical team believed a Broviac device was necessary because it would allow for more frequent access, to administer the many medicines required, over an extended period. The Broviac would be implanted into his chest via a surgery within the next month or two.

In the meantime, Doctors installed a PICC line (used for long-term intravenous antibiotics, nutrition, medication and blood draws) into his arm bedside. Even though they used numbing medication and pain relievers, it was quite unnerving to see Frankie extremely uncomfortable. By now, it was about 2 a.m. Frankie was crying again and agitated, and they decided to give him morphine to quell the pain. A few minutes later, Frankie was calm and looking at me with a drunken smile. "Wow, I feel nice now," he said. "This stuff is great."

I left Keri and Frankie at the hospital that night, and I collapsed in my bed at 3:30 a.m. About 4:45, I awoke in a panic and was sweating. I had dreamed that Frankie's cancer was back. Breathing heavily, I turned over to look at Keri. She wasn't there. I then realized I'd had a nightmare, except it was real. I also remembered that it was Father's Day. I had never felt more depressed.

For most of the day, I was numb. Somehow, I managed to break the news of Frank's relapse to Max, now 14, and James, now 16, without breaking down. I explained he would have a bone marrow transplant to save his life. They were disturbed by the cancer's return but had greatly matured and were better able to handle it.

Plans for Father's Day 2014 had been expected to be carefree. Keri had given me a deep-tissue massage gift certificate. With Frankie expected to be in the hospital for at least four months, I knew I had better get the massage now and salvage part of my

Father's Day. So, I scheduled a session before I returned to the hospital that night. The masseuse worked on me for 90 minutes; I have to admit it felt good.

As I prepared to leave, he tried to upsell me on more massages.

"I can give you a package of eight massages for the price of four?"

"No, thank you," I replied, knowing that the next 12 months of my life were going to be anything but predictable.

He pressed. "I can give you four massages for the price of three."

"No," I said. "I am all set."

He became fidgety for a moment and then blurted out: "I give a lot of massages in a week, Mr. Dezell. I have never seen a person with as much tension in their neck, shoulders and body as you have. You are extremely tight. The muscles in your shoulders are so tight. You can use several more sessions."

I said pointedly, "There are reasons why I am tense. I'm not going to get into it. Thanks for the massage. I'm all set for now."

Max, James and I ordered some burgers from a place near our house and then we took them to the hospital. By the time we got there, the burgers were cold and tasteless. That entire day and evening felt much the same.

It was all rather surreal. We had already been through this. James and Max tried to cheer up Frankie. Doctors were giving him large doses of steroids in advance of the chemo regimen that was scheduled to begin the next day. He was cranky and agitated.

Members of the hospital staff who had remembered him the first time stopped by to say hello. I was grateful that none acted alarmed or surprised at his return because that would have bothered him. We tried to make the day as normal as we could. There was definitely a lull in our psyches.

Keri mentioned that Dr. Levine had stopped by a few times and had expressed concern about my state of mind. She indicated that my feigning to punch a wall the day before had frightened her; she thought I was going to knock the wall down. Dr. Levine came by the room after our stone-cold dinner, and I pulled her into the hallway.

"Happy Father's Day," she said to me somberly.

"Thank you," I replied. "Keri told me that you were concerned yesterday that I was going to punch down some walls?"

"Well, I saw you pretending to punch some of them, and I knew how tense..."

"Jennifer, I know I am a little crazy in a good way, but I am not going to punch out the wall of a hospital. I was just trying to vent a bit and let Frankie know we had another fight on our hands. You don't need to worry about me."

She expressed relief.

I added: "I got a massage this afternoon for Father's Day. The guy who gave it to me said he had never seen anyone as tight or tense."

Dr. Levine understood.

I continued, "I am not going to punch out any walls, but I will tell you this. I have been through a tremendous amount in life, far more than you will ever know, and I can tell you that I am angrier right now than I have ever been in my life."

I started to cry, and her eyes welled up.

"Frankie was playing lacrosse last weekend. He got a haircut and looks so good. He was jumping on the trampoline on Friday, and this fucking cancer came back, and it's coming at him…and it's coming at him hard."

Dr. Levine was trying to control her emotions as tears streamed down her cheeks.

"I know you are more of a scientist and a scholar," I said through my sobs, "far more than I will ever be, and this…four years ago, this was a battle…it was a battle that you and he won."

I was crying hard, and I touched her shoulder.

"Now…it is a fucking war. And mark my words, this stupid, shitty cancer will not take my boy."

"No, it won't," she said.

"As I told Frankie yesterday, we will hit this with everything we've got. Four years ago, we did it in a gentlemanly way. Now, it's a street fight. You have always known me as a funny, jovial guy. But my attitude, my posture and my focus have changed now. I am changed."

My voice gained strength. "Cancer will not take my boy and I will put everything I have, and every ounce of my being, into making sure of that."

I gave her a hug and went back to Frankie's room.

The day sputtered to an end. Keri took the two other boys home, and I ended Father's Day 2014 spending the night with Frankie. He slept on the futon because Keri had made it safe and comfortable for him. Just like the first time around, Frankie didn't want to sleep in the hospital bed because it reminded him that he was sick. So, I climbed into it instead.

On Monday, the hospital was abuzz with activity beginning at 7 a.m. The hospital's rhythm always changed dramatically from the weekend to a weekday.

I watched Frankie asleep on the futon and decided that the shock and somberness we were feeling needed to cease. It was time to again face reality and make this relapse as radical, as positive and as zany of an experience as we could.

I need to praise the kindness, empathy and compassion that so many of the nurses and doctors exhibited. They knew another regimen was required and were responding pragmatically. This was quite comforting.

Someone once asked what it was like for Keri and me and our marriage, encountering childhood cancer twice. Candidly, we had no plan or strategy of what we were doing, especially the second time around. We made it work because she is the ying to my yang.

Keri is loving, personable, nurturing, strong and engaged. I am more intense and was laser-focused on taking care of Frankie and the rest of the family. I also knew the healing that came with humor, so I was determined to find ways to keep our family laughing. We both respected what each of us brought to the situation and knew that while our marriage was sometimes strained and our priorities were altered during these periods, it would bounce back because we both had the same goal in mind: to keep Frankie alive and to keep our family intact.

Morgan Stanley Children's Hospital staff told us that more than 60 percent of marriages fall apart when confronted with a sick child. We were not going to let that happen. Even though we didn't talk about it, Keri had the same mindset and posted an update a week after the relapse:

ROUND TWO....
Journal entry by Keri Dezell — June 19, 2014

I am at a loss for words- because there are none. This shouldn't happen ONCE to ANYONE, let alone a CHILD and TWICE??? How do you reconcile that? I guess we'll have to figure that out...

Frankie was readmitted to Morgan Stanley Children's Hospital on Saturday and was diagnosed with Acute Lymphoblastic Leukemia with markings for Burkitt's Leukemia (a rare combination). Purposely, I didn't make that point known last time around. Although I know it tried to bully us into believing the rarity held power, I thought NO way. That point is irrelevant. We will not feed the bully. BUT THIS TIME, since it had the audacity to show its ugly face again, WE WILL CALL IT OUT BY SPEAKING ITS NAME and WE WILL SHOW IT who's running this show: GOD, FRANKIE and US!!! NOT IT!

We do not have all the specifics, but the general picture looks like this... the induction phase will be a lot like last time. He'll be in hospital to begin with for about 35+ days. During that time, he'll be administered a variety of chemotherapies to help rid his bone marrow of ~~cancer~~, as they prepare it for a Bone Marrow Transplant.

Once released home, he'll continue to be in/out of hospital to receive additional chemotherapies, then radiation, then the Bone Marrow Transplant... so without a doubt, it's going to be a LONG HAUL. We are on our knees asking for GOD's Mercy and his complete healing for our baby, our FRANKIE.

At this moment, we don't know a lot of things, but we do know this... WE WILL NOT COWER. WE WILL WIN. Please PRAY, PRAY, PRAY, PRAY, for Frankie's safekeeping, his health, his continued progress, his spirit and his strength... and do not let up. Chemotherapy treatments will begin tomorrow... it will get harder before it gets easier, so we need your prayers.

FRANKIE'S TEAM! FRANKIE'S TEAM! FRANKIE'S TEAM!
It's round two people-let's KICK this ~~CANCER~~'s A$$!!!!!
With love and in prayer,
Keri, Jim, James, Max and FRANKIE!!!!

Frankie's followers from his CaringBridge site were in horror and disbelief. The responses came pouring in from all over the country:

Tammy Jenkins | June 20, 2014
Keri, You don't really know me... I am a business acquaintance of Jim's. I followed your previous journey and prayed for you and with you along the way. My heart is truly burdened for you and your family as I sit here weeping as I read your post. As a mom of three, I can only imagine what you are going through. I am in awe of your strength then and now. I will continue to pray for and with you and your family. God is not done with Frankie... HE is building the most amazing testimony in such a young life. May God be with you and bless you in this journey!
Bless the Lord, O my soul; and all that is within me, bless His holy name! Bless the Lord, O my soul, and forget not [one of] all His benefits—Who forgives all your iniquities, Who heals all your diseases. Psalm 103:1-3

Therefore humble yourselves under the mighty hand of God, that in due time He may exalt you, Casting the whole of your care [all your anxieties, all your worries, all your concerns, once and for all] on Him, for He cares for you affectionately and cares about you watchfully. 1 Peter 5:7

Do not fret or have any anxiety about anything, but in every circumstance and in everything, by prayer and petition, with thanksgiving, continue to make your wants known to God. And God's peace which transcends all understanding shall garrison and mount guard over your hearts and minds in Christ Jesus. Philippians 4:6-7

The Regan Family | June 20, 2014
Life is a team sport. And this team will do anything for its captain, Frankie Dezell. Rest up and punch back Frankie, as you always do.
Punch Back.

Lori Lichtenberger | June 20, 2014
Our dear, beautiful Frankie not only are we thinking of you and praying for you constantly, we are also asking everyone we know and sort of know to do the same! I started talking with a very nice man on my flight today and he told me he was going on a mission (in San Juan). It ends up that he is the pastor, so I asked him to keep you in his prayers. We even prayed for you on the airplane today. His name is Wayne Sibrava from Living Water Baptist Church in Owego, N.Y. So we will continue to do this every day until the entire world is praying for you!! Cancer has NOOOOOO idea who it is dealing with, but it will! We love you SO much and know you will win this battle! If you need any help

with your armor just let us know!! I am sure Robert has an oil can around here somewhere. XOXOXOXOXOXO

A few days after Frankie was readmitted, I had to speak at a work conference that was held at Dartmouth College in Hanover, New Hampshire. Hanover is a rather difficult place to reach. I wanted to cancel the trip, but it would have had a negative impact to pull out this close to the session.
I flew there in a daze and my mind was on Frankie as I drove around the mountains of western New Hampshire. Keri called me during the drive, and I quietly said to her, "You know, I am in the car, and I am driving around these twisting mountain highways trying to get to Dartmouth. And I keep thinking to myself that I would be more than willing to drive off one of these cliffs and kill myself in return for Frankie being okay, and not have to go through this again." Keri understood, because she felt the same.

Word spread through our town and Frankie's school that he was ill again. Hundreds of students made him cards and posters. Keri collected them all and hung each tribute on his hospital walls and ceiling. Within a week, his room looked like a banquet hall on New Year's Eve; Keri would have it no other way. Every ounce of positive energy, thoughts and prayers was going to surround him each day. Painfully, I went another route. I became laser focused only on Frankie and destroying his cancer. I grew introverted. I was extremely angry at God and stopped going to church. I knew that God and I would interact at another point, but for now I needed some space.

The initial focus of the treatments was to prepare Frankie for a bone marrow transplant. For the first month, doctors hit him hard with the chemo regimen and it did become a bit mundane. To keep Frankie engaged and active, we hung an indoor basketball hoop and I bought a Nerf football to play catch each day. Frankie would hang the hoop on the outside of his door, encourage nurses and other young cancer patients to play, and teach them how to shoot. It was inspiring to see the other sick children share some joy with him.

Our game of playing catch quickly became stale and boring, so we shifted the parameters by throwing the Nerf football as hard as we could at one another and seeing whether we could catch it. If you bumbled or dropped the pass, you were penalized a point. We trained the young new doctors and residents how to play our spontaneous game. They were surprised at how much velocity a Nerf football could muster.

After a few weeks, we continued to dance around the ugliness of the chemo and steroid regimens Frank was enduring. Helping us forge through were charitable groups that brought hope and cheer.

One remarkable charity was The Hole in the Wall, founded by the late actor Paul Newman. The group sent a couple of college students who visited Frankie weekly for 2 hours each time, and he had a blast. The moments they spent each week were so special and meaningful to him. They'd play video games, board games or simply talk and laugh for hours.

Nevertheless, as positive as we tried to make everything each day, the grim realities of Frankie's situation and the unknowns settled in.

One day, Frankie ran his hands through his hair and large strands fell on his shoulders; his hands were filled with clumps. The nurses recommended that we shave Frank's head quickly to avoid the itchiness and discomfort. As I ran the clippers across his head, Frankie sobbed. Despite the basketball games, the Nerf football contests and other daily distractions, the repeat of losing his hair couldn't be ignored and Frankie had to grasp that, once again, he was sick. It broke my heart. I hugged him as he cried and tried to reassure him.

To address Frankie's cancer once and for all, a specialized team of doctors and nurses would handle Frankie's bone marrow transplant and consult with Dr. Levine as needed. It was all rather elaborate and somewhat frightening. We'd have two-hour sessions with the team, and they would explain the risks, ramifications and protocols of the transplant.

The doctor in charge was an internationally renowned specialist named Prakash Satwani—brilliant, intense, quirky and with a good sense of humor. Each session with the Bone Marrow Transplant (BMT) team was exhausting, but I think the doctors appreciated our directness and questions as we tried to do what was best for Frank.

The new protocol and strategy would involve intense levels of chemotherapy. Once the evidence of cancer was minimal, doctors would then give him powerful levels of radiation before the transplant. At times, the BMT team meetings would last for several hours. And for the transplant to be successful, we needed to find a donor match. Dr. Satwani suggested that we have Frankie's brothers tested because sibling donors have a 25 percent chance of being a perfect match (which is preferred). Parents are the least favorable donors because the most that their marrow can match their child's is 50 percent.

Keri had a long talk with James and Max to see if they were okay with participating. Without hesitation, both agreed.

It was appropriate that Keri had the conversation with them because if I had taken the lead, I simply would have ordered them to do it and they would have no choice in the matter!

So, Max and James had their blood drawn and tested. In a stunning outcome, BOTH brothers' marrow matched Frankie's—a rare feat. The doctors were ecstatic, and we joined their glee.

Unfortunately, James' bloodwork showed that a walking mononucleosis virus was still dormant in him, and his marrow could not be used for fear it would transfer to Frankie's fragile immune system. So, Max was the preferred donor.
The brothers were jokingly competitive about it, and Max kept bragging that Frankie was going to get "Maxified." Frankie was hopeful that he would get Max's martial arts skills and kidded that had James been a match, he would absorb James' "smarts."

His doctors decided to administer a variety of chemotherapy to Frankie until they could decrease the cancer cells in his bone marrow to zero, or to a fraction of a percent. The lower the number, the better the chance that his new bone marrow would remain cancer-free.

After a month of chemo and radiation treatments, they tested Frankie's bone marrow for cancer cells through another glamorous aspiration, but still found small traces. Therefore, the doctors decided that another round of chemo was necessary.

Before proceeding, they allowed Frankie to go home between regimens. As we were packing to leave the hospital, Dr. Satwani came in to talk with us. During the middle of the conversation, he stated:

"You know, I have come to realize that you Dezells are a crazy family," he said, grinning. "You are all funny and have a great deal of energy. But I must be honest and tell you, you all curse and swear a lot. I have never met a family who swears like you do."

I looked at Dr. Satwani and smiled.

"So, you think we swear a lot?" I asked.

"Yes, you are like a group of sailors," Dr. Satwani replied.

"Well, you know what I think?" I asked. "I think you can take a fuck fly to the moon."

Dr. Satwani started laughing hysterically. "You see...you see."

I continued, "Over the past four years, our boy has been diagnosed twice with cancer. We have and will continue to do everything to keep him alive. Keri's and my marriage is still intact. Neither of us is drinking heavily or wasting away in depression. The one area of our lives that has unwrapped is our swearing. But as they say, until you walk in our shoes..."

Frankie was released on a Monday, and I commuted to my New York office for a few days. On that Wednesday afternoon, I got a call from Keri.

"So, you're going to think that I am crazy..." she began.

"I already do think you're crazy, but continue," I replied.

"As you know, my sister, Erin, was planning on having her wedding in late August."

"Okay," I replied.

"Well, she and Steve [her fiancé] will not have a wedding if Frankie can't be there."

"Okay."

"So, we're thinking of having the wedding this weekend."

"What? That sounds a little rash," I responded. "Where are they going to have it?"

"In our back yard. We'd do it in our back yard here in New York."

I balked.

"Keri, we just got out of the hospital after a month. You're exhausted. I am tired. Why are we going to have a wedding in our yard, and why this weekend?"

Keri had it figured out. "Frankie will be going back in for another round within the next 10 days. Once the transplant occurs, he'll be in isolation for three to four months. Outside of right now, we don't know when Frankie can be there. And Erin and Steve won't get married without Frankie. This weekend works. We can borrow chairs, we can have friends help set it up and bring flowers. It can be done by a justice of the peace."

I thought to myself: *Our lives are so screwed up and insane right now. Why not do something even crazier?*

"Okay," I agreed. "This is insane, but WTF."

We then needed to find someone to marry them. Keri reached out to our Town Hall. The role then became hotly contested. Four magistrates wanted the job. We ended up with the town's clerk.

I took the next two days off, mulched the gardens, pressure-washed the house and patio, and got the yard ready.

Early Saturday morning, I heard our dog barking and saw out the window a group of Keri's closest friends in our yard with flowers, decorations, chairs and runners.

I was quite touched to see how all these people rallied together for our family, and for Frankie.

The wedding was magnificent. The groom joined the wedding ceremony via a zip line. With only a day's notice, our family's favorite restaurant, DiNardo's, catered the event. Bridal march music was pumped through outdoor speakers. Keri's entire family was in attendance. But most important, Frankie was there, helping them celebrate the happiest day of their lives.

After the wedding, Frank was readmitted to the hospital for his next round of chemotherapy. It hit him hard. Although the cancer cells had diminished to 0.81 percent, it still wasn't enough. Frankie's doctors wanted to see those numbers even lower. Therefore, we went back home for a few days to let him recover before facing yet another round.

After he was readmitted, Frankie remained in the hospital for close to a month. We were then given a one-week hiatus. Never one to miss any opportunity, I asked the doctors if we could kidnap Frank again and take him to Cape Cod. They were hesitant, but I assured them that we could get him to Dana-Farber if anything went amuck. They agreed, and we rolled up there for five days. We went to drive-in movies, Frankie's favorite ice cream shop, and did crabbing from the rock jetties at the beach. It was the perfect break.

Upon his return to the hospital, Frankie was walloped again with chemo to get the cancer cells down to zero or 0.01 percent. The level remained at 0.81 percent, but the doctors were encouraged. Frank would have to undergo another session of chemo before the bone marrow transplant was scheduled, so we went home again for a few days as he recovered. It was like a zany merry-go-round and déjà vu all over again.

As the potential transplant date neared, we had several meetings with the oncologists, nurses and the BMT team. It had been four months since Frankie's relapse, and we were days away from the transplant date being set in stone.

Keri and I were exhausted when it was time for yet another formal meeting, this one quite intense. Three doctors, four nurse practitioners, nurses and social workers were in the room with us, but not Frankie. For almost two hours, the doctors advised us again of the risks, the potential problems, the side effects, the ramifications, and possible issues after the transplant.

We listened intently and Keri took notes. There was nowhere near the typical joking and banter that we usually had. The tone was far more serious.

Once the BMT team had finished the overview, the floor was open to questions. Neither Keri nor I had any. The doctors and nurses looked at one another in stunned silence. Then Dr. Satwani spoke up. "In all due respect, I am surprised that you two are so calm."

"What do you mean by that?" I asked.

"Usually, when we finish these sessions with people...they're distraught. Parents are crying and leaving the room. A lot of people can't take it and are depressed. I've gotten to know you both over the past few months, and I know you are both smart and compassionate people. I know you understand what we've said. I am just surprised you are both just sitting there."

"Well, what do you want us to do?" I said.

"As I said, every other parent we have had this conversation with is usually distraught and sobbing by the end of these meetings. I feel you both capture everything that has been said, yet you two are not showing any emotions at all."

Keri and I looked at one another and burst out laughing. We laughed uncontrollably. I'm sure it was a combination of delirium, determination and strength. I'm also sure it seemed highly inappropriate.

The BMT team was flabbergasted. I finally spoke up.

"Prakash," I began, "first things first. We have had a lot of meetings with you and your team over the past few months. I can assure you...we understand and fully comprehend everything that you went over. Thank you for this."

"That said," I continued, "in our house, you can cry if you are happy. You can cry if you are sad. You can cry if you're touched by something. But we don't and will not cry out of fear."
I paused for a moment.

"This is the second time in four years that cancer has tried to kill our son. It's time that we destroy it. We know that it has been, and is going to continue to be, a complete shit show getting to that point. But it's time to _**kill**_ cancer, once and for all.

"And I don't mean to be rude or dismissive when I say this about other people's reactions, but we're not going to get Frankie or ourselves through this by getting depressed or crying."

At this point, we were DONE with meetings and dialogue: It was time to close down this cancer saga once and for all.

Later that night, Keri prepared to update her blog and asked me to repeat what I had said. For all my machismo and bravado at the hospital earlier, I burst into tears when I had to say it again. So much for not crying!

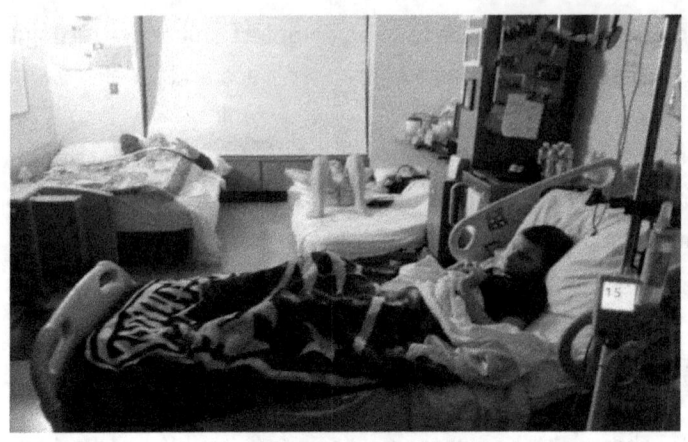

After the relapse, our family remained a united front. Frankie missed his home and family, so we brought it to him and had sleepovers in the hospital. Nurses turned a blind eye while chuckling, as we assembled beds. Keri's (the photographer) not pictured.

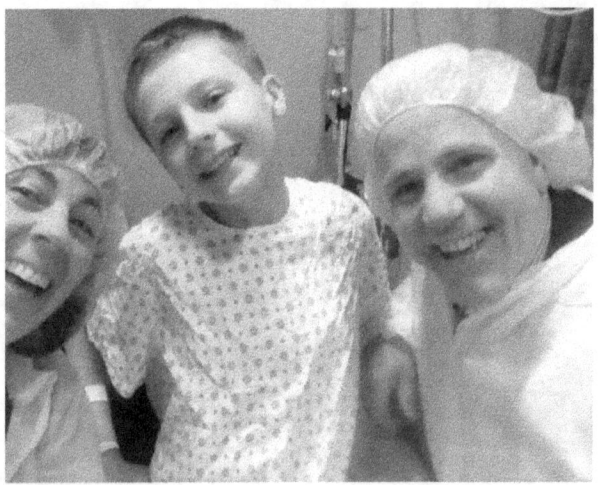

Working to bring some levity to yet one more bone marrow aspiration and spinal tap.

Killing Cancer And Getting "Maxified"

The next day, test results showed that the cancer cells were down to 0.01 percent, and the transplant was approved. It was scheduled for October 7, 2014—a date that was etched into our minds. Our back-and-forth cycle continued, and we went home for a few days before Frankie was readmitted for the final round: more chemo and radiation, and then the transplant with Max's bone marrow.

The night before Frankie was readmitted, we ate at his favorite restaurant. Keri and Frank took one car, and James, Max and I were in another. Frankie knew the next few months were going to be hell. On the way home, he expressed hesitation to Keri. "Mom, I don't want to go home. I don't want to go home to sleep and then wake up and have to go back to the hospital. Let's forget it, Mom. YOLO [you only live once], Mom! YOLO! Let's drive to California!! Let's just go! YOLO, Mom!"

Hearing his powerful words and seeing his eyes twinkling, Keri saw the glare from the streetlights bouncing off his hairless head. With tears in her eyes, she said, "Frankie, I get it. I truly do. I would give anything to be able to drive to California with you right now, at this very moment. I hear you loud and clear. YOLO is right, Frankie! But right now, so that you can have _many_ more YOLOs, we can't do that. We have to go to the hospital tomorrow to be sure we get you well and cancer-free—then YOLO it is! I promise you, Frankie, we're going to take a road trip to California, but for tonight, the backstreets of Bedford and Pound Ridge will have to do. Okay?"

With music blaring, windows down and the sunroof open, Keri and Frankie drove around singing their hearts out, allowing themselves to be lulled into the belief that this was just another normal, summer, carefree night. Pulling into our driveway two hours later (we live 10 minutes from the restaurant), a laughing, twinkly eyed and rejuvenated Frankie and Keri could be heard singing to Taylor Swift's song "Shake It Off":

"But I keep cruising
Can't stop, won't stop movin'
It's like I got this music in my mind
Sayin' it's gonna be alright...

"I never miss a beat
I'm lightnin' on my feet
And that's what they don't see, mm mm
that's what they don't see, mm mm...

"Cause the players gonna play, play, play, play, play
And the haters gonna hate, hate, hate, hate, hate
Baby, I'm just gonna shake, shake, shake, shake, shake
I shake it off. I shake it off (hoo-hoo-hoo)...
"I, I, I, shake it off, shake it off
I, I, I, shake it off, shake it off
I, I, I, shake it off, shake it off
I, I, I, shake it off, shake it off
I, I, I, shake it off, shake it off
I, I, I, shake it off, shake it off
I, I, I, shake it off, shake it off"

No coincidence there.

Out of all the crap we had been through and witnessed over four years, including more than 33 spinal taps, nothing could prepare us for the horrors of what was coming. Our lives went beyond a "shit show": This was a fuck flight straight into hell.

Before taking Frankie to the hospital, we went to his favorite delicatessen in Harlem. The deli owner loved him and used to give him free sandwiches. He prayed for Frankie all the time.

Frankie was pretty banged up from all the chemo and didn't have a lot of energy. After lunch, Keri and I were transporting his luggage, our bags, computers, and everything else we needed for the next phase. As we walked down a side street, two men from a nearby shelter—who appeared to be drug addicts—spotted us, our luggage and our other bags. They approached us with a look that indicated they wanted to mug us.

I couldn't believe it. Here we were with a 12-year-old cancer patient—pale, bald and about to get a bone marrow transplant—and these two fools wanted to rob us, or worse.

I put the bags down to free my hands and fists. I then glared at the two of them. They looked up from the bags to me and determined we were not the right people to mug that day. They dispersed and, most likely, saved their own lives. I am not a violent person. However, these guys must have seen in my reaction that we were prepared for battle, and it was not the day to be picking a fight with or mugging my family.

After we checked in to the hospital, we witnessed a sense of urgency that I had never seen before. Doctors immediately

administered chemotherapy to Frankie to help prepare his body for the upcoming three days of full body radiation.
Throughout the four years that Frankie fought cancer, he had experienced a lot of grueling reactions and procedures with chemo: nausea; hair loss; vomiting; mouth ulcers and sores; significant weight loss; pain; complications from anesthesia; dozens of spinal taps and bone aspirations; bloating and other side effects from steroids; nerve damage; and joint pain.

Later, he'd have complications from graft-versus-host disease (GVHD). However, nothing had prepared us for the radiation regimen. It was more savage than I could have imagined.

The Radiation Department was built for adults. It was not set up for 12-year-olds. The room was formidable and reflected the serious nature of its purpose—to destroy cancer.

We were brought into a 30-by-30-foot concrete vault, and a 5,000-pound lead door sealed shut behind us. Doctors explained that extensive prep work was necessary to accommodate Frankie's size. Radiation equipment had to be re-positioned over several days of "dry runs" to keep Frankie's body safe from gamma rays.

The actual radiation machine was massive and daunting. It was positioned directly across from some weird contraption that looked like a medieval torture chamber. Frankie was to sit on what looked like a bicycle seat during the radiation sessions. His torso would be compressed between two small plexiglass shields to protect his lungs and other vital organs. Radiation beams would be transmitted from the machine through airwaves landing directly on Frankie—hitting every inch of his still growing 12-year-old body. Frankie received full-body radiation for three consecutive days, twice a day.

Once Frankie was situated in the radiation room, Keri and I would leave the vault along with all his doctors, nurses, radiologists and technicians. Small video screens would allow us to monitor his status in the vault, but he could not see us. He could only hear us through a speaker system. We made several playlists of his favorite songs to distract him. On September 29, 2014, the first session of radiation started.

Frankie was pinned between the shields, with his arms hanging by his sides. Shortly after the radiation started, we could see his pale skin turning gray. He endured radiation for several minutes. Then we heard his weak and quivering voice plead with us to make it stop. In complete and utter horror, we watched (over the video screen) his body go limp. We thought he was dying and became frantic! Doctors immediately ceased the radiation and pushed a button to unseal the door. After waiting for what seemed like an eternity, the 5,000-pound door slowly opened. Frankie's head was hanging over the front shield. He looked like a rag doll.

Doctors, technicians and nurses scrambled to release him from the device. As soon as he was free, he started to vomit violently and was carried to a wheelchair. Nurses checked his vitals to confirm nothing was life-threatening. The staff determined that the prophylactic medicine he was given to combat radiation nausea was too strong. This is what caused his rapid deterioration.

After just a few minutes of rest and some sips of water, Frankie regained some strength. The medical staff began to relax, but Keri and I were beside ourselves and began to question everything. Conflicted, we still knew we had to convince Frankie that he could do this. We needed him to understand that if he wanted to live-he had to do this. As he stared at his feet, he absorbed our words. He then raised his head, looked us square in the eyes and with fierce determination and a steady, calm voice, he said, "Okay. Let's do this. It's go time."

For three consecutive days, two times a day, repeatedly, he withstood what Keri and I both felt we never could. My respect for Frankie had increased immensely over the years as he fought cancer. It had now magnified tenfold. Keri and I agreed that had we endured even one hour of what he went through those days, we would have gotten off that seat, gone home and let cancer kill us. It was that horrific.

To make matters worse, when the full-body radiation was completed, a now weakened and sickly Frankie started a four-day chemo regimen that required he be given three showers a day. This was necessary to counteract the chemo being used during this phase; once secreted through his pores, it would cause severe burns if left on his skin. Keri and the nurses applied prescription lotions to his body several times a day to deter blistering and burns.

As he lay in his bed one night, Frankie was lethargic while the nurses and Keri applied lotion and wrapped him in special blankets trying to make him comfortable. He looked half-dead. At one point, our eyes met. I saw his fill with tears, and his body and lips quivered in pain. I knelt next to him, held his hand and told him how sorry I was, that I wished I could absorb his pain. It was agony.

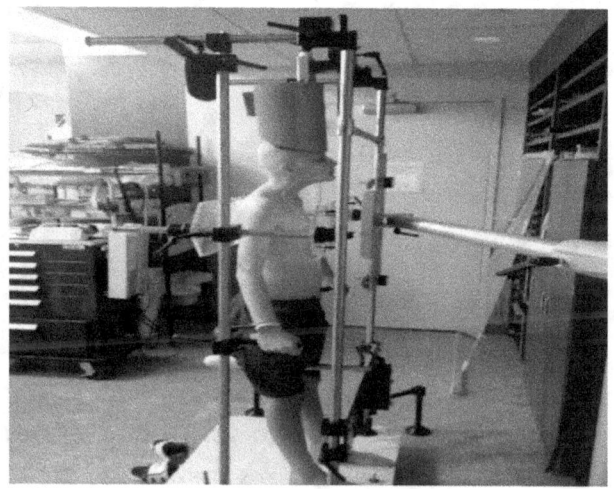

Prepping Frankie for the radiation chamber took many hours over several days

We watched Frankie over the monitor while he was inside the radiation chamber. Undeniably, it was one of the most disturbing weeks of our lives.

With the radiation and chemo rounds over, 14-year-old brother Max arrived for the bone marrow transplant. Frankie continued to give Max advice and "pointers" on how to handle the anesthesia. Typical older brother, Max ignored most of it—which he later regretted.

Early on the day of the transplant, Keri shared the latest developments in her journal.

It's GO TIME....
Journal entry by Keri Dezell — Oct. 7, 2014

This past week was a very rough and tough week for Frankie...this is why you're just hearing from me.

Unfortunately, due to the current time (1:30 a.m), I'm not able to elaborate on that further, but hope to fill you in later.

The purpose of this update is to call on each of you for your continued support, love, good vibes, positive energies and prayers. Please send them up into the heavens and out into the universe for our Max Man and Frankie's safekeeping—a hundredfold.

At approx. 7:30 a.m. today, Max will be put under anesthesia and doctors will perform the bone marrow harvest (strange name we agree!! This is the procedure when a large/long needled is inserted into Max's back to collect bone marrow from his hip). Max's procedure will take approx. 2 hours. After the procedure, Max will need to stay in the hospital for 24 hours for additional support and monitoring. At some point this afternoon, the actual transplant will occur. During this time, Frankie will be closely monitored and will have his Doctor, a Nurse and a Nurse Practitioner standing by his bedside. Unfortunately, Frankie will feel much worse before he feels better. He will remain in the hospital (in isolation) for another 4-6 weeks while his body responds to the new bone marrow. It is another grueling and difficult process that Frankie will be made to endure. Again, I hope to explain this in more detail later, but for now...

Please pray for both Max and Frankie's safekeeping.
Please pray that Frankie's body receives Max's bone marrow without ANY complications.

Please pray that Frankie's body does not reject Max's bone marrow, but instead receives it as the strong and healthy marrow that Frankie's body needs to live. Please pray that Max's marrow takes over and rids Frankie's body of this rancid ~~cancer~~ FOREVER AND EVER.

Please just pray the words that you know are deep within my heart, but at this moment are lost.

Thank you in abundance for your continued support, love and prayers. Means the WORLD TO US.
XOOXXOXO
Keri, Jim, James, Max and FRANKIE!!!

Karen Warren | Oct. 7, 2014
See Jesus' magnificent energy. Watch Jesus transfuse Frankie with His holy and clean cells and watch it flow throughout his body as Jesus lays hands and covers him with His cleansing blood. We should all visualize this picture. Amen.
We are all with you, Frankie.
Much love and prayers from the Warrens

William Harrington | Oct. 7, 2014
Frankie, just to let you know that you were in my thoughts and prayers all day today. I hope you got to see the Pats play this past Sunday. I am sure you did. Tom Brady, who was coming off a bad loss, played like an animal and kicked butt. Today you played like him. And I know you will fight harder than him to get better. Always think about you. Could not be prouder. Be well and Godspeed.
Max, you are the coolest, bravest, most caring and unselfish

person I know. I am so proud of you and to be your friend. You have set a wonderful example for everyone and a very high bar to match. Feel better bud. B

Darlene Iacovino | Oct. 7, 2014
Thank you for the post, was literally just thinking about all of you. The Holy Spirit is at work! Praying, Praying and Praying!
Darlene

As ideal as it was having a sibling match for Frankie's bone marrow, no one ever whispered to Keri and me about the fine print of having two of your children undergoing life threatening procedures at the same time; it was one of the most fucked-up time frames of my life.

That morning, doctors and nurses continued to prepare Frankie's body, giving him aggressive prophylactic medicines. Then it was time to take Max to the surgery room. However, Frankie was getting violently sick from the medicine, and his nurses (who remained by Frankie's side) were calling to advise us.

Later, in Max's operating room, having our healthy boy's hand go limp in our fingers as the anesthesia knocked him out was petrifying. Surgeons used 8-inch needles to extract the 5 million cells that they hoped to acquire from Max's bone marrow. His marrow was then rushed to Frankie's bedside to start the transplant.

Max was in surgery for a few hours and in recovery a few more. When he regained consciousness, he felt sick and was in terrible pain. Max (the No Cursing Treaty creator) tends to be the most courteous and respectful of our three boys, so to hear him barking orders at nurses and demanding pain meds was comical. "You're too slow," he told one nurse. "I am so sick of this shit." Keri and I had to laugh.

Our day had started at 6 a.m. By 4:30 p.m., the transplant was over. Max was back in Frankie's hospital wing in recovery. Frankie was still knocked out by the cocktail of meds. Keri and I both looked like we had been hit by a train and were sitting quietly in Frank's room. Dr. Satwani entered and announced that the transplant was a success.

"Everything went great. Max was a fabulous donor. We got over 11 million cells. You should be very happy."

Looking closely at me, he added: "But, you look terrible!"

At this stage, I didn't care and was so fatigued but grateful.

"Since June, everyone has been raving about how 'rare,' 'wonderful' and 'fantastic' it is that Frankie's brothers could be donors," I told him.

"However, in that beautiful 'BONE MARROW TRANSPLANT' brochure that no one showed us and that doesn't exist, no one listed in the fine print what it is like for a parent to have *two* of your children undergoing aggressive and life-saving surgeries *at the same time*.

"Prakash, I have lived through a lot in life, but that was undoubtedly the most fucked up 10 hours I have ever been through."

Keri and I then decided to get some sleep. She retired to Max's room and I stayed with Frankie.

Meanwhile, James posted a beautiful note to his younger brothers on Instagram.

"There are no two people in the world that I would want to call my brothers. Today marked a turning point in this exhausting and awful battle against Frankie's second fight with leukemia. Today, Max was successfully able to transplant his bone marrow to help fight and defeat Frankie's leukemia. Max, the amount of courage and bravery you have shown throughout this process is unbelievable and your willingness to be Frankie's donor without hesitation is extremely admirable. Frankie, you truly are the most amazing person I have ever met on this earth. There has been no one, that I've ever seen, go through cancer twice, stuck in a hospital for months on end, being sick and lose their hair after chemotherapy, often too sick to get out of bed, having to go through many blood transfusions and spinal taps, be able to stay as upbeat and happy as you have. There is not a single kid in this world that could've endured what you have and keep that gleaming smile on your face. Your spirit is like nothing I've ever seen. You're an inspiration not only to me, but the entire community. When I look at you, you have the character and toughness that I'll strive and try to attain throughout my entire lifetime, but that you've already achieved at 12 years old. When the 2 months of isolation and

you're being away from everyone is over, I'll be waiting for that spirit and million-dollar smile to return home. I'll be there to tell you you're truly 100% cancer free. That's the day when you'll have finally killed this horrific illness that has consumed 4 years of your childhood—and you'll be able to say, this time without hesitation, "I'm a survivor." When that day comes, I'll be watching you with admiration and in awe, knowing that you're someone who has gone through hell and back and still managed to stand tall on his feet. I've loved you since the day you were born and held you in my lap, and I will love you till the day I rest in peace. But for now, we need to focus on the next two months. I know you'll get through it somehow or another and FUCK CANCER UP. See you at home cancer-free in two months. I love you."

In one of the oddest displays of seismic trickery, the day after the transplant Keri came down with a nasty flu-like cold. This banished her from the hospital because Frankie's immune system was literally at zero. How disturbing is it that two of your sons undergo serious medical procedures together and one gets a bone marrow transplant and you are forbidden from seeing him?

In early October she posted:

A long and winding road that we BELIEVE will lead us to a rainbow... Please GOD.
by Keri Dezell — Oct. 9, 2014

Tonight:
For those who live in the area, a healing Mass will be said for

Frankie at 7 PM this evening at St. Patrick's Parish, State Road, Bedford, N.Y. We would deeply appreciate any and all praying hearts and hands. If you are not able to attend, please hold a moment of prayer for Frankie on your own, anytime between the hours of 7-8 this evening. Let's bombard the heavens with our healing intentions for Frankie...We're so grateful to have you to call on. THANK YOU.

To better understand where we are now, I think it's important to know where we've been. In June, when it was discovered that Frankie relapsed with the same exact ~~cancer~~ as before (Acute Lymphoblastic Leukemia with markings for Burkitt's), a Bone Marrow Transplant was almost immediately put on the table. Why? Well, Frankie relapsed 4 years after the initial diagnosis in 2010, which told the medical team that the chemo regimen received last diagnosis worked (which I know sounds confusing because his ~~cancer~~ returned), but I'll explain further. From the medical team's perspective, if the chemo regimen from the last time didn't work, Frankie would have relapsed during the chemo regimen (a bad thing) or a lot sooner than four years out from the initial diagnosis. Having said that, the fact that the ~~cancer~~ found a way to return despite the chemo regimen in 2010 shows that Frankie's marrow is determined to produce ~~cancer~~ cells. Since that's the case, the most effective way to shut this ~~cancer~~ down is to replace Frankie's bone marrow with Max's marrow. However, studies show that bone marrow transplants are most successful, and have less risk of relapse, when healthy marrow (Max's marrow) is put into "sickly marrow" (Frankie's) that has little to no ~~cancer~~ remaining in it (any number showing ~~cancer~~ cells of .01 percent or under w/the ultimate number being ZERO) at the time of transplant. Obviously, as you know, Frankie's doctors were pleased because after the third chemo regimen they reached a number less than .01, allowing them to move forward with the transplant. Let it be known that although the number didn't reach zero, this is another example of finding the right balance...where the risks to bring his number closer to zero (by of hitting him with more chemo and radiation) would outweigh the benefits. Meaning, if they continued to hit him with more chemo, it was more likely that Frankie could become less sensitive to the effects of the chemo, allowing the ~~cancer~~ to get stronger and/or he could suffer more long-term side effects and/or organ damage from the chemo, hence the decision to proceed with the transplant.

On Tuesday, October 7th Frankie received Max's bone marrow via the "transplant." For Max that meant going under anesthesia for 2+ hours, while doctors used a needle and inserted it multiple times into his hips via his back to withdraw the marrow. They needed to retrieve approx. 5 million cells via the "harvest" and ended up with 11 million! That a boy, Max!! So the cells they didn't use will be stored and frozen, but our bets are that we will never need to use them ever again!! Now, the actual "transplant" process was pretty anti-climactic as it literally looks like a blood transfusion. Meaning a bag of Max's marrow is hung on Frankie's IV pole and it is transfused into him via one of his Broviac lines. However, due to possible and serious complications that could have arisen, he had a nurse, a nurse practitioner and his BMT doctor by his side for the 3 hours it took for the marrow to be transfused. Thankfully, his was a pretty "uneventful" and BLESSED transplant. Thank you, GOD! However, it's important to note that although the transplant has occurred, we're not out of the woods and may not be for quite some time. Aside from the horrors of last week's radiation/chemo and its subsequent side effects (that I have yet to explain) which continue to plague him; the list continues to grow, as Frankie's body adjusts to receiving Max's bone marrow as its own. Due to the multitude of complexities involved with a bone marrow transplant, Frankie will be closely monitored and continues to be given a variety of prophylactic medicines to help prevent infection and/or damage to his liver, his kidneys, his heart, his lungs, etc. Frankie will remain in isolation and will only be able to visit with HEALTHY and suited-up (wearing masks, gloves and cover-ups) immediate family members because he has NO IMMUNE SYSTEM and won't for some time. Something as small as a paper cut could prove troublesome or deadly. Another concern that he'll need to be monitored for is something called Graft Versus Host Disease...

> Graft-versus-host disease (GVHD) is a complication that can occur after a stem cell or bone marrow transplant in which the newly transplanted donor cells attack the transplant recipient's body.

To help prevent this from happening, Frankie was given a drug called Tacrolimus. In most instances, patients in Frankie's predicament are given two different drugs to help combat GVHD. However, for Frankie it was decided that the initial plan (if necessary, could change) would entail Frankie being given one drug, Tacrolimus. The Tacrolimus aids Frankie's body to view Max's marrow as more of a friend than a foe, so it would accept it rather than fight it; having said that, we *don't* want

Frankie's body to be so comfortable with Max's marrow that it looks at it like its own and therefore finds a way to produce more ~~cancer~~ cells. Hence the reason for them to use only one medication to protect him against GVHD instead of two. Pretty complicated across the board.

Aside from the above, to use Jim's words, Frankie is the toughest human being we've ever met. There have been many times that Jim and I have looked at one another because we feel so helpless and unable to bring Frankie relief from the disconcerting process he must undergo to save his life, that we wonder if we could "hack" what he does, over and over again?

This is a grueling, painful, exhausting, constant juggling act that we've been told will only get worse before it gets better. For these reasons, do not let up with your positive energies, love and prayers. GOD is listening...we feel it.

About 6 p.m. on Tuesday, when all was said and done, Max is ushered into room 519 while Frankie remains in room 504....

With a smug like look on his face, Max calls Frankie via facetime and the exchange goes like this...
 "So, Frankie, how's does it feel to be me?"

"I don't know yet, Max. It's only been an hour. I need more time."

Then a little later in the evening, when Max is feeling a tad bit better, Max pops in on Frankie and says...

"Hey, Frankie, I didn't like that anesthesia at all, man."

"I told you not to take the mask, Max. I told you to take the IV. You should have listened to me. You made a rookie mistake for sure."

Lolly Quagliarello | Oct. 9, 2014
Thank you Keri for this detail filled update—for, as we fervently pray for Frankie's successful BMT and in turn putting him on the path to recovery, these updates bring us out of the darkness for a while. Our family prays day and night for Frankie to kick this insidious disease's butt! He is beyond measure the most brave warrior I have ever met--and he's only 12 years old. What a MAN... Your family's deep faith and love for each other is keeping you all buoyant during this awful nightmare. We love you all soooo very much~ and I will continue to light a candle anytime I pass my church in NYC... Here for you always/anytime, day or night. Love, prayers, and hope for Frankie- and all of you! xoxo

Gail Doyle | Oct. 9, 2014
Lifting Frankie up in prayers to Our Lord.
Keri, Wish I could be at Mass but will definitely be praying for your "Super Hero." God give you the strength you need till Frankie is completely NED. [No Evidence of Disease] Here for you. xoxoxoxoxo Gail

Aunt Ellen | Oct. 10, 2014
Those comments are hilarious! I'm laughing and crying at the same time. God Bless Frankie, we are keeping him in our prayers

and reading all the details so we can pray fervently and nonstop. Love and Hugs, Auntie Ellen

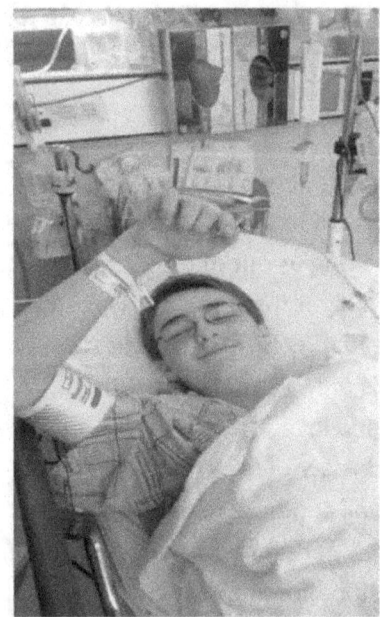 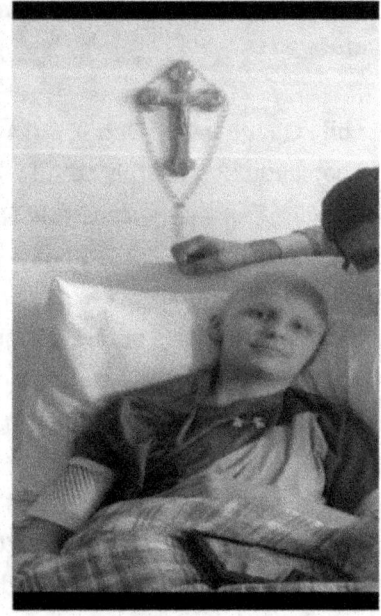

Frankie's life was saved by his older brother, Maxwell. This said, having both children undergo life-threatening procedures at the same time almost killed Keri and me.

As Keri announced in her post, two days after the transplant our church held a prayer service for Frankie. He had become so well-known and inspirational, and so many family friends were there, that the church was standing room only. James was the only one from our immediate family who could attend. We knew many people would be craving information and insight about Frankie, Max and the procedure. We asked James to provide an update at the end of the service, but he felt nervous. To sway his fears, I told him that he didn't have to write a speech or prepare anything.

"Well, then, what should I say?" he asked.

"Read the Instagram post you wrote to your two brothers," I replied. "Just don't curse in church."

It tormented Keri that her nasty cold prevented her from being at the hospital. So, for nine long days just Frankie and I were stuck in isolation. I worked remotely, so it was quite taxing for the both of us. Frankie had several side effects from the transplant, including the dreaded GVHD. He couldn't control his bowels and his nausea was amplified. I must have changed his bedding at least three times a day. He had no appetite and developed neuropathy, which is damage to the peripheral nerves.

Frankie remained in isolation into November. No one except doctors, nurses, Keri and I were allowed in the room 24/7. We all had to wear special gowns and goggles.

The quarantine affected Frankie's positive outlook. He didn't want to interact with friends, not even to play video games. He had tremendous pain in his hands and feet from the neuropathy. He sometimes had to sleep sitting up while his hands and feet soaked in tubs of cool water to numb some of the pain.

After five months spent mostly in the hospital, he was sick of being sick. He was depressed, and it broke our hearts. The only positive moments came from his New England Patriots' winning streak, which thrilled him. I kept telling him about a future filled with fun. I would talk about riding roller coasters, going on vacations and seeing Broadway shows. He would listen and not respond. About five weeks after the transplant, one of his nurses came into the room and began unplugging his IVs.

"You two want to get some fresh air?" she said with a smile. "You want out of lockup?"

It was just the boost Frankie needed. We dressed him in a hat, coat gloves and surgical mask. His IV pole worked temporarily on batteries, so we secured the IV lines on it. It was a heavy pole, with lots of IV bags, equipment and shelves to hold his numerous medicines.

To avoid others and ensure a safe environment, we used the back elevator to whisk Frankie downstairs to the courtyard behind the hospital—where Keri, James and Max were waiting to surprise him. Frankie was ecstatic. It was a beautiful day, and I pushed his massive IV pole. We had been allotted 45 minutes, but we stayed for well over an hour. I was grateful that Frankie could feel the warmth of the sun. Amid his hat, coat, gloves and surgical mask, all you could see were his beautiful blue eyes. After five hard weeks of pain, misery and isolation, his eyes were twinkling.

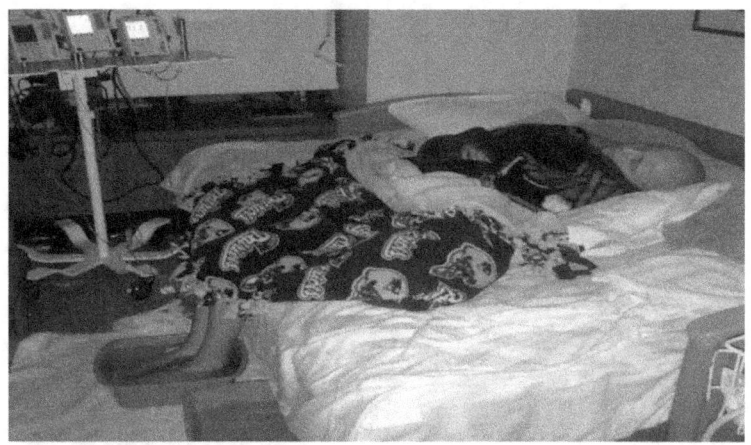

Post-transplant: In isolation for over 100 days, Frankie is beset with many GVHD symptoms.

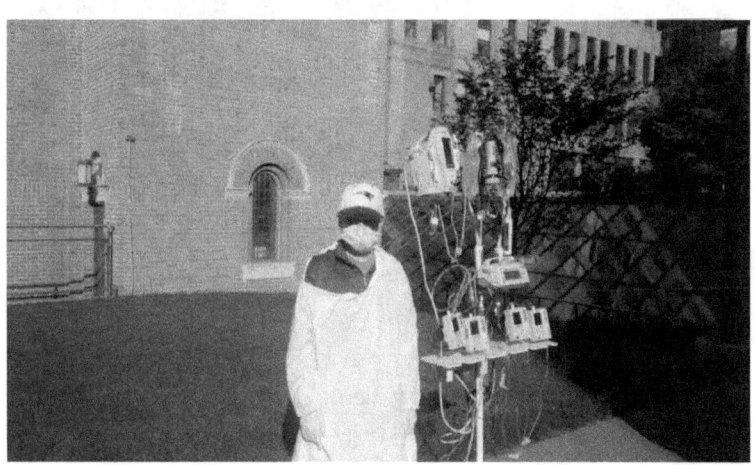

During those 100 days, Frankie's only companions were his parents and his IV pole full of the medicine that kept him alive.

And, finally, after several weeks, his brothers are permitted to visit him.

A few days later, the hospital gave us permission to leave. It again felt like we were paroled from prison. We had a lot to pack up and used numerous carts to push everything outside. Frankie had to bundle up as usual and wear protective gear and masks.

At home, Frankie excitedly sat on our kitchen floor for 15 minutes playing with our beloved dog, Malcolm; they had missed each other terribly over the past seven weeks. Frankie could not stop laughing as Malcolm jumped on him again and again, licking him.

Keri waited a few days before updating her blog.

On 11/12, after 45 days in "Lock Up" our beautiful FRANKIE returned HOME…. THANK YOU GOD!! THANK YOU!!

Journal entry by Keri Dezell – Nov. 25, 2014

Yes, you heard it right. I am so sorry for not making this announcement until today. Honestly, I didn't even make phone calls. When we were told that they were looking at a possible discharge date of 11/12 and having come through the craziness we had just experienced, then having watched a prior discharge date come and go, topped off by not seeing a "well enough" Frankie in front of me when they proposed this discharge date…I said to myself, "I'll believe it when I see it."

Low and behold on 11/12 our Frankie joyously returned home. We didn't realize we were in a competition with who missed him most… happy tears were flowing. Click on link below…

https://www.youtube.com/watch?v=GYnq-cxfHUc&list=PL9KEwDELpo1X20YE7Jp2HQgp8SH9y6USB

So many of you have reached out quite concerned because there's been no word and/or because I've been so quiet... it's hard to explain, but I texted one friend what I think sums up where we are and why I've been so quiet:

"Love you too and I'm sorry. These last couple of weeks I've had to pull away from everyone because it's just been way too much of everything. I almost can't explain it and am too tired to even try. I have minimal energy, and the energy I do have I'm focusing it on Frankie and our other cuties. Having said that, I haven't been able to pick up the phone or write a CaringBridge entry because every moment of our day I'm CONSUMED with keeping Frankie safe and/or performing my new nurse duties: 4 times a day meds, flushing and care of his Broviac lines, changing dressings as needed, 2 nightly IV hookups and weekly clinic visits and so much more.

Frankie's medical team (rightfully so) has imposed all kinds of restrictions meant to keep him safe and infection-free, hopefully keeping him out of the hospital while his bone marrow recovers (I'm told that's almost impossible, but we're going to do everything we can to prove them wrong!). Overall, Frankie's tired but he's doing great. I just need to keep it that way—so right now he's the boy in the bubble and I'm nonstop w/nursing duties to keep him and all things around him sterile. Including the other oh-so-happy-to-have-Frankie-home-germ-infested-cuties returning from school each day!! In the door they come, up the stairs directly to the shower they go!! ha ha!"

Okay, so where are we? In general, most Bone Marrow Transplant patients have their first bone marrow aspiration (remove a sample of the recipient's bone marrow to determine what percentage of their marrow is converted to the donor's and checking for any applicable diseases) on day 100 (meaning 100 days out from transplant). In Frankie's case because his

~~cancer~~ WAS :) so rare, Dr. Satwani feels it would be prudent to check Frankie's marrow on or around days 30, 60 and 90. As you're aware, Frankie already had Day 30's bone marrow aspiration- thankfully, it showed that Frankie's marrow was ~~cancer~~-free!!! Hallelujah! Thank you GOD! It also showed that 99% of Frankie's blood type/cells are now Max's. The next bone marrow aspiration (Day 60) is tentatively scheduled for December 8th. At that time, Dr. Satwani would like to see the obvious- continued ~~cancer~~-free results and for Frankie's marrow to be 100% of Max's. Based on Frankie's recent progress, he has no reason to believe otherwise, so this remains our present hope and our prayer.

The last time around, the first five years were the most critical. Meaning, if a patient was going to relapse, they would most likely do so within the first five years of diagnosis. Unfortunately, and as you already know, Frankie relapsed close to 4 years out from his original diagnosis, creating the need for the Bone Marrow Transplant. Considering this, please know that after a bone marrow transplant the **FIRST YEAR** is the most critical. Data show there is a 40% chance of relapse with the FIRST year. However, because Frankie's ~~cancer~~ is rare there's no data and/or percentages to look to, hence the need to follow him more closely than most. ***It is equally important to note that Dr. Satwani is pleased with Frankie's progress thus far! Gooooooo FRANKIE Gooooooo!!! Please GOD may this continue.

At present, Frankie will continue to make weekly trips to the clinic for close monitoring and medication changes, etc. Because his immune system is so fragile and immature, he is quite susceptible to picking up infections/viruses that most of us fight off without a beat, each moment of every day. Therefore, Frankie's diet is restricted to a low-microbial diet, and he's not able to be in public places, in crowds or with anyone other than us. Hard on him for sure, but so much better than being in isolation in the hospital. Having said that, we SO APPRECIATE and LOVE each member of the medical team that surrounded and cared for us. We wouldn't be home if it weren't for their devotion to keeping Frankie safe and well. We KNOW THIS TO BE TRUE. THANK YOU!! THANK YOU!! THANK YOU!! :) Now, may the reluctant and newly anointed neurotic nurse, aka Mom, do all in her power to keep our Frankie home! PLEASE GOD. So much gratitude for continuing to choose to share in our journey by holding us up in prayer and/or with positive thoughts... may the many blessings we realize we have been gifted, even amid our obvious trials (a gift unto itself), be felt by you and yours this Holiday week and ALWAYS. With love, XOXOOXOXX

Keri, Jim, James, Max and Frankie!!

Home at last. Malcolm was thrilled to have him back.

Just a few last-minute gifts for Frankie to take home from the hospital.

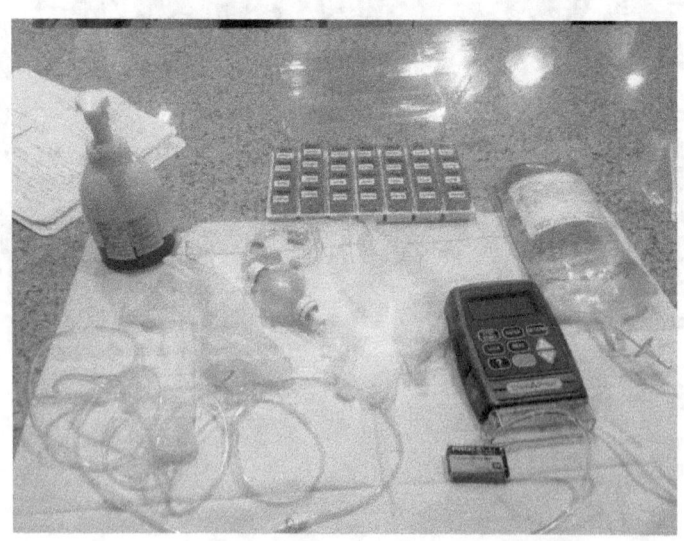

Frankie was not allowed to have any visitors for 100 days. Precautions were also in place for any of us who had to venture out in public. As Keri mentioned, James and Max had to shower after school each day before they could interact with him, as did I after returning from work. For fear of any food contamination or meals not being properly cooked, he was not permitted to eat anything made outside our home. We learned how to make pizza and many of his favorite soups. We had a quiet Thanksgiving with just the five of us. It was a bit surreal, but we were so grateful to be together and have him doing okay.

Despite our gratitude that he was alive, Keri and I were quite conscious of all that Frankie was missing due to the cancer. He was unable to attend normal basic activities like school- or social activities like birthday parties, bar/bat mitzvahs and spring formals/dances. He couldn't play on his school's football team or his CYO basketball team. It was painful for him and us. About 120 days after the bone marrow transplant, he attended (as a spectator) one of his CYO team's basketball game and asked me if he should wear his old jersey. I told him that he shouldn't. He was puzzled for a moment, and I replied, "Instead of wearing a jersey, why don't you show up in a shirt that says 'I Destroyed Cancer Today. What Did You Do?" Frankie liked that idea.

As Keri continued to write her blog and interact with close friends and family, I, on the other hand, became further detached. I did not want to see people. I did not want to reach out to anyone. In the free time that I had, I took our dog for long walks in the woods.

Despite all the love and compassion we received from so many people, some inconsiderate individuals are so egocentric that they can be downright foolish. At one point, an obnoxious acquaintance who was a bit intoxicated confronted me. He chastised me that "no one ever sees you anymore," people were annoyed because "you don't go anywhere or talk to anyone" and I was "reclusive and anti-social."

I was irked by the person's comments and knew alcohol was fueling most of it. I finally responded tersely.

"It is true," I said. "I don't go anywhere. I primarily stay at home with Frankie and my family." I glared at him. "My son has been diagnosed with cancer twice in the past four years. I do not mean to be rude or abrasive when I say this, but I don't care about anything else other than getting him well."

"People wonder where you are and why you don't reach out…" he protested.

"I don't reach out because I don't want to. Who is going to help me right now? Who knows what it is like to have a kid diagnosed with cancer once—let alone twice? I appreciate people's concerns, but I don't want to talk about it. I don't want to answer the same questions over and over again of 'How's Frankie?' I don't want the sympathetic looks. I could handle it the first time around, but I'm over that now. I am only focused on Frankie. Every weekend, I take my dog deep into the woods, where no one can see me, and I don't have to see anyone else. And I walk for as long as I can. If people don't understand or like that, I don't care. All that I care about is Frankie right now."

I then turned and walked away.

The doctors at Columbia continued to monitor and evaluate Frankie. Because his form of cancer was so rare, Dr. Satwani decided to go an "extra 3,000 miles" in terms of having his marrow evaluated after each lumbar test. Normally, Frankie's lab results were evaluated at Columbia (which could evaluate 10,000 cells) and then at Johns Hopkins Hospital in Baltimore (which could study 100,000 cells). Dr. Satwani was not convinced this was enough, so his bloodwork was also sent to a more technically advanced lab in Seattle that could assess more than a million cells.

As Christmas approached, our typically large dinner party with friends and family on that night was scrapped. It was just the five of us.

To break the monotony of our isolation, Keri's sister indicated that we might be in for a "surprise" one night. There were rumors that she had hired Christmas carolers to serenade us. Lo and behold, at dusk one evening some of the worst Christmas singing I had ever heard invaded the silent night. Not only was the singing out of tune, lacked harmony and contained garbled words, there were strong Boston accents coming from the carolers. I thought that my sister-in-law should get her money back because the singing was that awful. As they got closer to our house, I realized the "Carolers for Hire" were not professionals, but Keri's entire family. Over 20 of them drove from the Boston area, about 200 miles away, just to sing to Frankie and the rest of the Dezells. It was quite touching.

The Wildest Group of Christmas Carolers ever assembled...aka our family from Massachusetts.

Shortly after Christmas, doctors permitted Keri's parents to visit us because they're retired and their exposure to others was minimal; we made a feast for them. While I was exhausted, annoyed and still a bit on edge with God, I slowly and cautiously began returning to church. Our relationship was progressively healing.

Meanwhile, Frankie's New England Patriots kept winning and we rolled into 2015 with a complete focus on health and happiness. The Patriots went on to win Super Bowl XLIX in quite a wild fashion. Keri posted a video of our family screaming like lunatics over the Pats' championship, 28-24, over the Seattle Seahawks.

F-R-A-N-K-I-E's been waiting his whole life for this...
Journal Entry by Keri Dezell — February 1, 2015

FRANKIE WILL WIN... JUST LIKE HIS TEAM...
http://youtu.be/iZ6f5sEdMtY

For those of you who have seen the video... OMG can you imagine this family's reaction in a crisis? Baaaahahahaha!!!

FRANKIE WILL WIN!!

The remainder of Frankie's winter 2015 consisted of continued home-schooling as tolerated and monthly hospital visits for checkups. Initially, his health news continued to be positive. Then, something shifted.

In the five years that we had battled Frank's cancer, never once was I afraid. I knew that faith, love, laughter and the medical community were going to take care of it. But in April, six months after the transplant, a surprise development left us crippled in fear.

Frank's most recent bone aspiration, in March, was sent to the three usual institutions: Columbia, Hopkins and Seattle. Seattle's results came back with an "A+" stating that no cancer cells were present. Hopkins' outcome was the same. However, Columbia's test was "flagged" to indicate that Frankie's cancer had returned for a gut-wrenching and unbelievable third time.

When we heard the news, I felt the whole Earth shudder. As dynamic and brilliant as he is, Dr. Satwani was listless and disillusioned when he called us. He explained that the only solution now was for a cutting edge, intensive, new T-cell transplant, and the only hospital near us (at that time) that could manage the procedure was Children's Hospital of

Philadelphia (CHOP) in Pennsylvania.

My mind was on fire. We would need to sell our home at a large loss and move to Pennsylvania. We would need to take the other two boys out of school. The financial pressures of treating cancer—even with good health insurance like ours—are overwhelming. I contemplated whether I should file for bankruptcy. It had been arduous enough financially managing this twice. Dealing with the costs a third time, in another state, was impossible to grasp. I lay awake at night for days wondering how we were going to manage it.

Dr. Satwani had said during our call that he would probe the matter further. For over a week, Keri and I were the only two who knew about Columbia's positive leukemia test. We just couldn't tell Frankie. Really, how could we? After several days, Dr. Satwani reached out said he wanted to speak with us at 4 p.m. on that coming Friday; it was about a week after Frankie's 13th birthday. Keri did not want to take the call at the house because Frankie could overhear and he'd know something was amiss. We went for a drive and decided to go to our church, where we lit candles. We then got back into our car, parked behind the church, and waited.

Right on time with the call, Dr. Satwani sounded fatigued, but a bit more relaxed than during our previous conversation. Before he could explain the reason for our talk, however, he was interrupted and put us on hold for a few minutes.

Keri and I sat in my truck in tortured silence, paralyzed with fear. When the doctor returned, he explained that Frankie was okay.

With wide eyes, Keri and I looked at each other. FRANKIE WAS

OKAY!!!

"We did some further investigating of Columbia's results. Because of Frankie's relapse, his bloodwork gets extra scrutiny and evaluation. A lab technician was alarmed about one issue, but upon further review by me, Dr. Levine and the head of oncology at Columbia—it's all good. The results from Seattle and Hopkins are accurate."

We were stunned and remained silent as the million-ton anchor was lifted from our shoulders. I thanked God repeatedly. The overwhelming stress had disappeared in one fell swoop.

Insanity Is Powerful Medicine

Despite all the obstacles over the course of defeating Frankie's cancer, there were humorous events that kept us grounded and sane. One time, Frankie, Max and I were at a Home Depot and the boys got into a spat about something. Max, annoyed at Frank, muttered: "I can't believe that I saved your life."

A woman behind me heard the exchange, made eye contact and started to chuckle.

"Are they brothers?" she asked.

"Yes," I replied.

"Well, that line was a little dramatic," she said.

"Which one?" I asked, because I had been only half-listening.

"When the older one said that he had 'saved' the other one's life."

"Well," I replied, "I'm not going to get into the whole story, but he <u>actually did</u> save his life."

The woman pushed her cart past us with a quizzical look.

As autumn 2015 approached, we took advantage of everything we could. I kept my promises to Frank and took him to Broadway shows and amusement parks. We didn't waste a minute.

Keri provided highlights in her CaringBridge journal.

Hmmm...
Journal Entry by Keri Dezell — August 29, 2015

I BELIEVE IN THIS...

AND THIS...

AND THIS...

Columbia Spinal Fluid- negative, NO ~~CANCER~~
Columbia Bone Marrow (reviews 10,000 cells) – Negative, NO ~~CANCER~~
Johns Hopkins Bone Marrow (reviews 100,000 cells) – Negative, NO ~~CANCER~~
Adaptive Biotechnologies Seattle (reviews 1,000,000 cells) – Negative, NO ~~CANCER~~

I realize I could have closed this entry leaving you with the info above and most would have been satisfied. However, if I did, it would only be half the story...and the fact that you're still here, five years in, following our Frankie and our family tells me that you want and deserve more than that. It is for this reason that I share the following perspective.

It's so strange how time and experience can change things. Let me please first acknowledge how INCREDIBLY GRATEFUL we are to hear the words ~~cancer~~ free. Through too many painful experiences, we realize how profoundly invaluable these words are and as a result, are extremely thankful for the BLESSINGS we're living today. However, we've also come to acknowledge that these words, although extraordinarily powerful at this moment, can be quite fickle...bringing us to our knees in thanks today and deep despair tomorrow. The words ~~cancer~~ free are not steadfast, nor will anyone, anywhere guarantee them, so in that light what do they really mean? I'm not sure what to make of them when they're constantly being challenged during Frankie's continued follow-up clinic visits, lab draws, chemo/radiation ramification follow-ups, bone marrow aspirations, lumbar punctures, intrathecal injections, etc..,

This may sound pessimistic or depressing and perhaps to some extent it is, but this is our reality and our truth. Therefore, WE CANNOT and WILL NOT GIVE these words that kind of power. The constant, and exhausting, challenge for our family is how to thrive despite such horrifying instability. Some days we do this with ease, while other days the emotional rollercoaster takes its toll and leaves us questioning everything and anything, including who the heck we are. But it is in these moments, GOD has ALWAYS provided us with the ability to see WHO WE ARE NOT. And THIS is what continues to push our FAMILY SUCCESSFULLY forward. Thank you, GOD, for these gifts!

So what does all this mean? Who the hell knows? Most likely it means that I'm a basket case in need of a straitjacket (which I think could be true regardless ha!), but I'd prefer to think that it means that words like ~~cancer~~ free although undeniably important, DO NOT BREATH LIFE INTO US- WE BREATHE LIFE INTO THEM. Therefore, WE WILL CONTINUE TO FEED and BELIEVE in not those words, but in LIFE, EACH OTHER, TIME and in GOD. It is our belief, if we can do this, regardless of where life takes us, there's no way we can go wrong. So, Words? Hmm...well, for now, they're not my favorite thing. Hence so much trouble writing updates.

A whole is greater than the sum of its parts- and our family, as long as we're believing and loving together, will ALWAYS win. Hands down.

Some additional notes on the medical front:

On 8/4 Frankie concluded a heart/lung function test. This provided us a "baseline" for Frankie's heart/lung function after chemo/radiation, etc.., Preliminary reports note that Frankie's lung function (although still not back to normal before chemo/radiation) has not deteriorated further since July's lung performance test. Thank you GOD.

On 9/10, we'll meet with Frankie's cardiologist to discuss the heart function test results from the test performed on 8/4. Then Frankie will have an echocardiogram to monitor heart disease and an EKG to monitor his heart rate. We're hopeful that all tests will show improvement or confirm no further deterioration in Frankie's heart function. In June, Frankie's heart function showed slight deterioration, but can be managed with medication.

On 9/10, we'll also meet with Dr. Satwani, Frankie's Bone Marrow Transplant doctor, and blood will be drawn and checked for continued bone marrow recovery and/or any initial signs of concern/~~cancer~~. We expect all will be well.

September is Childhood ~~Cancer~~ Awareness Month. It deserves all ADULTS' attention. We're the only ones that can make a difference. Children in general, let alone these desperately sick children, cannot be their own advocate. I obviously have a lot to say on this subject but for now am only choosing to say this...

WE NEED TO CREATE AWARENESS...
AWARENESS=FUNDING=RESEARCH=LIFE

If you're not the kind of person to march for a cause or to speak at a conference, I have simple solutions. Tell people about Frankie. Tell people that the GOLD RIBBON represents Childhood ~~Cancer~~ Awareness, so that the GOLD RIBBON can do for Childhood ~~cancer~~ what the PINK RIBBON has done for Breast ~~Cancer~~. Ask your school to have each of their sports teams wear gold socks for the month of SEPT., as our great friend Marisa did at her son's high school. Wear GOLD ribbons on your lapel the month of Sept., or year-round and when people ask you what it's for, tell them! Tell them it's for the "Frankie's of the world" and you are wearing it for the month of September for CHILDHOOD ~~CANCER~~ AWARENESS MONTH. Hang a GOLD ribbon on your place of business, home or get a GOLD ribbon car magnet. Be creative. Get creative.

http://www.choosehope.com/category/childhood-cancer-gold?filter_category%5B%5D=36

We so value your support, your prayers, your positive thoughts and your love—more than we could ever express and more than you'll ever know.

As always, an abundance of thanks for your continued prayers, support and love. XOXO Keri, Jim, James, Max and Frankie

In early September 2015, 11 months after the transplant, Frankie was invited to an event in Times Square honoring Pediatric Cancer Awareness. Times Square was illuminated in gold in recognition of childhood cancer. Frankie and Keri took the train into Manhattan to attend. Frank wore a shirt his Aunt Erin got for him after the transplant. She had recalled what I said to Frankie when he wanted to go to his team's basketball game. The shirt was black with words written in gold: "I DESTROYED CANCER TODAY. WHAT DID YOU DO?"

Enough said.

We were so excited to have Frank doing better each day. As the new school year began, Frankie was eager to attend classes.

He also decided to play football and we were thrilled for him. The coaches and athletic supervisor, however, were concerned and asked to meet with us. We explained that we took full responsibility for his decision and just wanted to give him the opportunity to deny cancer from robbing him of anything.

I tried to attend all his games. Even if he played only a couple of minutes, we'd cheer for him as if he'd won the Super Bowl.

In the last game of the season, I watched him play the defensive position of safety. He pursued a running back carrying the ball. Frankie missed the tackle, and the other player got around him. He then chased the player down the field, but could not come close to catching him before the player scored a touchdown.

Frankie walked to the sideline, unstrapped his chin pad and

lifted off his helmet. He looked at me in the stands. We both knew that he didn't stand a chance of tackling that kid. Frankie's body, coordination and stamina at this stage simply weren't there. We smiled at one another, understanding that things were different now. The two regimens of chemo and steroids, then the transplant and radiation, had taken their toll. Nonetheless, I was immensely proud of him and went down and gave him a hug. He seemed to accept that his world was now different, permanently. But he was alive, and he was happy.

October 2015: One year after the transplant, Frank is looking for some action on the field.

A Worthy Milestone

At the one-year anniversary of Frankie's bone marrow transplant with Max, Keri celebrated on her blog (and included the photo on the page prior):

Journal entry by Keri Dezell — Oct. 7, 2015
THANK YOU GOD for THIS BEAUTIFUL DAY.
"...those who wait for the Lord shall renew their strength.
*   They shall mount up with wings like eagles,*
they shall run and not be weary,
*   they shall walk and not faint." (Isiah 40:31)*

We are BEYOND BLESSED and OUR HEARTS ARE FULL.
May our BLESSINGS continue...
With Love and in prayer, Keri, Jim, James, Max and FRANKIE!

Suzie Payson | Oct. 8, 2015
This brought tears to my eyes, Keri. Tears of joy for all of you! I saw James at Scotts Corners and he told me how well Frankie is doing. So happy for all of you!! xo

Randi Aitken | Oct. 8, 2015
BELIEVE!!! Way to go Frankie and your entire family!!! This makes me smile!! F$&K Cancer!!!

The Brotmanns (Lisa, Matt, Sam & Lucy) | Oct. 8, 2015
Wow what a year it has been!! So glad to see the old Frankie again!! Love to you all!!

A few weeks later, Frankie had his final (I thought No. 34, but

Keri thought No. 29) spinal tap/aspiration. Keri wrote:

Here's to #29 going down and out without a hitch...
Journal entry by Keri Dezell — Oct. 26, 2015

As you're aware, Wednesday, October 7, 2015 was the one-year anniversary of Frankie's Bone Marrow Transplant aka MAX'S cells blasting the sh*t out of any residual ~~cancer~~ cells looking to take our Frankie down!!! That was a HUGE milestone!!!! Why?? Typically, if a patient is going to relapse, their risk of doing so is at its highest within the 1st year AFTER transplant. If the patient hasn't relapsed within the year after transplant, then the chances of a relapse occurring reduces SIGNIFICANTLY!!! WE BELIEVE with all of our hearts that FRANKIE WILL CONTINUE on the path of ~~cancer~~-free healing, but we must confirm that he is indeed ~~cancer~~ free through a bone marrow aspiration (take sample of his marrow & check it for ~~cancer~~ cells), spinal tap (withdraw spinal fluid & check it for ~~cancer~~ cells) and intrathecal (inject chemo into his spinal column to prevent ~~cancer~~ from finding a home there).

Tomorrow, October 27, 2015, Frankie's scheduled to have what should be his LAST bone marrow aspiration!! I don't have an exact count, but if I had to guess, tomorrow's aspiration will be Frankie's 29th!!

Why is this worth noting? This should be his LAST aspiration/spinal and chemo treatment FOREVER!!!!
Thank you GOD!

At this point, you could probably tell me this information

backward and forward, but just in case...samples will be sent to three labs:
Columbia- looks at 10,000 cells
Johns Hopkins- looks at 100,000 cells
Adaptive Technologies in Seattle- looks at 1,000,000 cells

All results should be back within two weeks. We expect results to confirm NED or NO EVIDENCE OF DISEASE. Frankie will continue to be monitored through the outpatient clinic via bloodwork and follow-ups, but he shouldn't have to endure ANYMORE PROCEDURES or CHEMO!!!! Please, GOD.

We realize how incredibly blessed we are to STILL have so many of you to call on. If you would please take a minute, or two or three or 100 :) and offer up your most positive energies and prayers for Frankie's safekeeping and continued free healing, we would be even more grateful. This has been an uncomfortable procedure for Frankie and the chemo doesn't help. Please pray for Frankie's comfort and swift recovery. THANK YOU so very much.

**** Frankie's most recent Lung and Heart follow-ups have shown no further deterioration! Any slight issues he's had have been controlled with medication. THANK YOU, GOD.

With love and immeasurable thanks,
Keri, Jim, James, Max and FRANKIE!!!!!

Frankie—The Walking, Talking Miracle Knucklehead

And here we are, in May 2022…12 years from when Frankie was first diagnosed. He is only 20 years old, and he's had cancer twice.

This cancer conqueror has ingested more medications and steroids than most people will ever need in a lifetime. He has handled more spinal taps and bone marrow aspirations than I can count and persevered through more than 32 cycles of chemotherapy protocols. He has undergone isolated and full-body radiation. He endured a bone marrow transplant with his brother. He has had multiple long-term hospitalizations, including at least 40 days in isolation, and has missed four-plus years of school. All this happened before he got his driver's license.

Cancer changed our family. Each one of us approaches life quite differently now. In many ways, this is good and we greet life passionately. In other ways, we're quite frayed and a bit fatigued. It depends on the day. It seems like each month since Frankie's transplant, there has been SOMETHING that creeps in and bites our family. Some of it has been as grave and intense as GVHD. Other situations have been a minor stomach bug at his school that all kids got for two days. But because of Frankie's compromised immune system, he got it for 10 days and lost 10 pounds.

Keri remains Frankie's dogged and steadfast Guardian Angel. She takes him to various doctor appointments for follow-ups to monitor and treat ramifications from chemotherapy and radiation (oncologists, pulmonologists, endocrinologists, cardiologists, neurologists, etc.). She tracks his medicines, watches his diet, and takes him to naturopaths to try to fill in the gaps the medical world appears unable to answer.

It can all be quite daunting after a dozen years, especially as we help guide him through his final three years of college.

At times, I've stepped back in the whirlwind of side effects and ongoing appointments to say to Keri: "A-H-H."

After she looks at me like she wants to kill me, I respond: "He is <u>A</u>LIVE. He is <u>H</u>APPY. He is <u>H</u>EALTHY."

We enjoy and are completely entertained watching him be our knucklehead son because that is, in its own way, amidst all the side effects of the treatments, a miracle.

July 2017, Dr. Jennifer Levine and Frankie

July 2018, Dr. Prakash Satwani and Frankie

Words cannot express the gratitude we hold in our hearts for each of you

The Costs of Eradicating Childhood Cancer

I have used a lot of negative adjectives to describe cancer and my disdain for it. Cancer is random. It is repulsive. It is unrelenting.

As a family, we feel it can be—and must be—thwarted. All those facing cancer need to be resilient, reckless and ruthless in their approach to dealing with it. Cancer feeds on fear and weakness; these emotions can never, ever be revealed.

I do not intend to be machismo in describing how we (or anyone encountering cancer) need to combat it. Anyone who has (or had) cancer and anyone who loves and cares for a cancer patient knows that facing it is a street fight that can last several years. You need to give it everything that you have. It is a bareknuckle, ugly and scarring brawl.

Cancer is overwhelming. Any person or family encountering it needs to **overwhelm it back**. We truly feel that love, laughter, courage and "being more insane than cancer itself" are as important to the healing and victory over it as the medicine and chemotherapy are.

As intelligent as Frankie's doctors are, and as grateful as we are to have the medical facilities near us, we also know other factors contributed to our success in defeating cancer. Such as:

- playing naked football in our yard
- watching R-rated movies with an 8-year-old
- having pillow fights in hospital rooms
- kidnapping Frank and going to Cape Cod
- having parties with 22 kids spending the night

- holding a wedding in your back yard while waiting for a bone marrow transplant.

Further, prayer, spirituality and honoring a higher power (no matter what you conceive it to be) were also instrumental in healing Frankie.

I spoke at a charity fundraiser shortly after Frankie was diagnosed, trying to raise money and awareness. There were several financial donors there and someone asked: "I have so many people and organizations asking me for money now—why should I give to this?"

I replied, "You heard me talk about my son, and how well he is doing?"

The person nodded.

"Thirty years ago, my son would be dead," I said bluntly. "The advancements in cancer care and cancer remediation have come so far, and it's because of charities like this one that this has happened. That's why you should give to this organization."

Much, much more needs to be done to eradicate childhood cancer and reduce the implications of treatment. From my own layman's point of view, cancer is remediated with poison. Chemotherapy and radiation are toxins, and their respective long-term side effects are brutal.

There must be a better way to approach this. Further research and funding are critical.

I witnessed Frankie and other cancer patients who, in many ways, are like veterans of wars. There are perennial side effects and ongoing issues with all of them.

Frankie has had lung and heart issues, cognitive functioning issues, learning setbacks, thyroid inconsistencies, muscle weakness, advanced bone aging and many other maladies post-transplant. He was diagnosed at one stage as having a neurological issue referred to as "Alice in Wonderland Syndrome" (distortions of visual perception, the body image, and the experience of time); significant weight loss from common colds and stomach viruses; extreme fatigue; and pertussis (whooping cough) that lasted over a month. He missed one-third of school days due to illnesses. Life isn't perfect, but Frankie is happy and alive.

Cancer treatments are archaic across the entire spectrum. Yet, for children facing the disease, medical care is even more outdated.

Cancer is a leading cause of death of children, yet statistics show that <u>less than 4 percent of all funding for cancer research wanders into the pediatric segment</u>. Cancer alters everyone's lives: For a child, it is beyond horrific, and ramifications from treatments (on their still growing bodies) last a lifetime.

Some issues show themselves at the onset, while others reveal themselves years later. Not to mention, there are sometimes secondary cancers caused by treatment used to extinguish the first. Surviving children are paying a high price.

More needs to be done to understand pediatric cancer, to reduce the number of cases and shrink the severity of side effects. And more also needs to be done to reduce the costs of treating it. We met a mother recently who lost her home while her daughter was in treatment because of the exorbitant bills. I estimate that our insurance companies paid over $4 million to treat Frankie's cancer. It had an out-of-pocket impact on our family of over $500,000 and I am floored by that. One antifungal medication cost $45,000 a month (thankfully, we had insurance!). According to the National Library of Medicine, the cost of childhood cancer treatment is close to $1 million per child. This isn't right, especially when all you want is your child to live.

We could not conclude without reiterating our special thanks to our families, friends and community for the support they provided. We truly would not have been able to get through this without their consistent outpouring of kindness and compassion. We are eternally grateful. We also highlight how important and magnificent it is when a community comes together to help those in need.

We'll also do one more shoutout to the charitable organizations that were there for Frankie through thick and thin. From the Lil' Bravest to Make-A-Wish and from Gift of Life to The Hole in the Wall Gang, your work and efforts were as integral to Frankie's success as the medicine he received. We thank God for you.

Go GOLD for September – Childhood Cancer Awareness Month.

More than 4%

And Life Comes Full Circle

In 2016 when our oldest son, James, was a freshman in college, a charity called Gift of Life visited his campus seeking bone marrow donors. At this stage, the mononucleosis that had thwarted James' wish to be Frankie's donor was no longer a factor. Knowing how important the transplant was to saving Frankie's life, James signed up and didn't think much more about it.

In summer 2019, Gift of Life reached out to him. James was a match for a 7-year-old boy suffering from leukemia. He took several days off from college and underwent a Bone Marrow Harvest procedure to donate his marrow to a child he didn't even know. Privacy issues prevent James from knowing the boy's identity or health for some time. He knew how critical the transplant was to save this boy's life. He said later that he would have become a donor even if Frankie had not been sick.

In May 2021, after some restrictions and limitations that were imposed by COVID-19 were lifted, and 11 years after he had been diagnosed, Frankie and Keri (who were both vaccinated) took the long-awaited journey from New York to California that they had planned the night before the transplant. They jumped in the car, cranked up the music and fulfilled this dream together. YOLO!!!

Childhood cancer may have reshaped our family's life. But, we live harder. We work harder. We love and laugh harder. We will never forget the amazing people along the way who helped and supported us medically, emotionally and spiritually. We are committed to the fight of bringing awareness to this illness and searching for ways that no child has to endure it again.

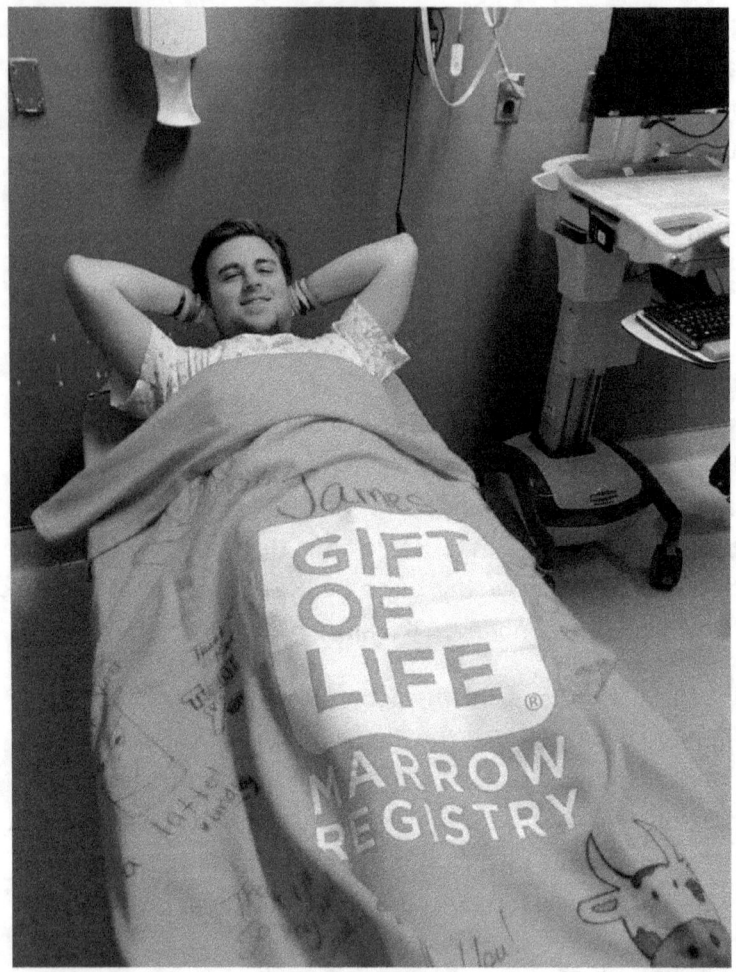

Frankie's oldest brother, James, would have loved to have been his donor, but a dormant case of mononucleosis prevented him from being a candidate in 2014. In October 2019, James was cleared to be a donor and helped save a young boy's life.

In 2021, after the COVID-19 lockdown was lifted and they were both vaccinated, Keri and Frankie took their infamous road trip from New York to California. YOLO BABY!!!!!!!

In Special Thanks and Acknowledgment

Without the assistance and kindness of the following people and groups, our experience throughout this endeavor, and our ability to finish this book, would not have been possible. While so many helped us, those listed below went "above and beyond," and for this we are eternally grateful. An extra shoutout of appreciation to my sister-in-law Maureen Conners Dezell for her careful editing of this book and to my sister Maureen Dezell for her time and effort editing the first draft. And to Alejandra Rodriguez for her creative assistance designing the book cover.

The Dezell & O'Brien Families	Father Joseph Domfeh
Grandma and Grandpa Blair	St. Patrick's Parish
Pam and "Pops" O'Brien	Meagan H. McQuade
Erin Langhorst	Paris Thomas
Ellen O'Brien	Brian "IJ" Geller
Dan & Jessica McNamara	Katy Rudy-Tomczak
Jennifer Santulli	Sue Novak
The Quagliarello Family	Diane McKenney
The Lichtenberger Family	Sally Green
The Novia Family	The Salvi Family
The Arkison Family	The Brotmann Family
The Harrington Family	The Fitz Family
Marisa Sullivan	The Shea Family
Valerie Price	The Giattino Family
The McNamara Family	Greg Manocherian
Chris Horgan	The Leva Family
The Silcox Family	Michelle (Murphy) Ham
Kathyleen and Curt McDonald	The Brown Family

The Maiarano Family
Dr. Todd Palker
The Mele Family
The Neary Family
Juan Gutierrez
Steve Sapiano
Kathy and Scot Jennings
Christina "Valet"
Prayers for Grace
Grace Group

Diane Kelly
Dr. Tony Wang
The Delli Carpini Family
Dr. Jason Davis
Nick Swisher
Jane Dunleavy
Gina "The Transporter"
Mary Ellen Lavelle
Prayer Warriors

And to the following organizations and their staff:

NYP Radiation Oncology and Staff
The New York-Presbyterian BMT Team
Richard Jacob Judy Memorial Fund
FDNY Engine 84/Ladder 34
CUMC Pediatric Hematology-Oncology staff
The Staff of DiNardo's Restaurant
"5 Tower" Pediatric Oncology NURSES at NYP
Tasty Deli, Washington Heights, NY
Child Life Specialists at Morgan Stanley Hospital
The Lil' Bravest Foundation
The Bedford/Pound Ridge Community
The Bedford Central School District
Center for Comprehensive Wellness at Columbia University

For further information, insight and interaction about the book, its authors and childhood cancer-- please feel free to visit our website:

www.idestroyedcancertoday.org

*With Love, Gratitude and in Prayer
James, Frankie, Keri, Jim and Max!!*

www.ingramcontent.com/pod-product-compliance
Lightning Source LLC
LaVergne TN
LVHW021819060526
838201LV00058B/3442